Instant Paper Airplanes

E. Richard Churchill
Illustrated by James Michaels

Sterling Publishing Co., Inc.   New York

For Rose and Melissa—May they always fly high

Edited by Timothy Nolan

Library of Congress Cataloging-in-Publication Data

Churchill, E. Richard (Elmer Richard)
    Instant paper airplanes / by E. Richard Churchill ; illustrated by
James Michaels.
        p.   cm.
    Includes index.
    ISBN 0-8069-6796-X
    1. Paper airplanes—Juvenile literature.   I. Michaels, James.
II. Title.
TL770.C49   1988
745.592—dc19   88-12325
                                                                    CIP
                                                                    AC

        4 5 6 7 8 9 10

Copyright © 1988 by E. Richard Churchill
Published by Sterling Publishing Co., Inc.
387 Park Avenue South, New York, N.Y. 10016
Distributed in Canada by Sterling Publishing
℅ Canadian Manda Group, P.O. Box 920, Station U
Toronto, Ontario, Canada M8Z 5P9
Distributed in Great Britain and Europe by Cassell PLC
Artillery House, Artillery Row, London SW1P 1RT, England
Distributed in Australia by Capricorn Ltd.
P.O. Box 665, Lane Cove, NSW 2066
Manufactured in the United States of America
All rights reserved

Sterling ISBN 0-8069-6796-X   Trade

Contents

Introduction

Folding and flying a paper airplane can be just as easy as one, two, three. All you need is a sheet of notebook paper, a few quick folds, and you're ready for your first flight.

Most of the paper projects in this book will need notebook paper. However, there's no reason why you can't use typing paper or duplicator paper (from the copy machine) instead. Keep this in mind as you build your paper air force. Now, let's get ready for take-off . . .

METRIC EQUIVALENCY CHART

MM—MILLIMETRES   CM—CENTIMETRES

INCHES TO MILLIMETRES AND CENTIMETRES

INCHES	MM	CM	INCHES	CM	INCHES	CM
⅛	3	0.3	9	22.9	30	76.2
¼	6	0.6	10	25.4	31	78.7
⅜	10	1.0	11	27.9	32	81.3
½	13	1.3	12	30.5	33	83.8
⅝	16	1.6	13	33.0	34	86.4
¾	19	1.9	14	35.6	35	88.9
⅞	22	2.2	15	38.1	36	91.4
1	25	2.5	16	40.6	37	94.0
1¼	32	3.2	17	43.2	38	96.5
1½	38	3.8	18	45.7	39	99.1
1¾	44	4.4	19	48.3	40	101.6
2	51	5.1	20	50.8	41	104.1
2½	64	6.4	21	53.3	42	106.7
3	76	7.6	22	55.9	43	109.2
3½	89	8.9	23	58.4	44	111.8
4	102	10.2	24	61.0	45	114.3
4½	114	11.4	25	63.5	46	116.8
5	127	12.7	26	66.0	47	119.4
6	152	15.2	27	68.6	48	121.9
7	178	17.8	28	71.1	49	124.5
8	203	20.3	29	73.7	50	127.0

YARDS TO METRES

YARDS	METRES	YARDS	METRES	YARDS	METRES	YARDS	METRES	YARDS	METRES
⅛	0.11	2⅛	1.94	4⅛	3.77	6⅛	5.60	8⅛	7.43
¼	0.23	2¼	2.06	4¼	3.89	6¼	5.72	8¼	7.54
⅜	0.34	2⅜	2.17	4⅜	4.00	6⅜	5.83	8⅜	7.66
½	0.46	2½	2.29	4½	4.11	6½	5.94	8½	7.77
⅝	0.57	2⅝	2.40	4⅝	4.23	6⅝	6.06	8⅝	7.89
¾	0.69	2¾	2.51	4¾	4.34	6¾	6.17	8¾	8.00
⅞	0.80	2⅞	2.63	4⅞	4.46	6⅞	6.29	8⅞	8.12
1	0.91	3	2.74	5	4.57	7	6.40	9	8.23
1⅛	1.03	3⅛	2.86	5⅛	4.69	7⅛	6.52	9⅛	8.34
1¼	1.14	3¼	2.97	5¼	4.80	7¼	6.63	9¼	8.46
1⅜	1.26	3⅜	3.09	5⅜	4.91	7⅜	6.74	9⅜	8.57
1½	1.37	3½	3.20	5½	5.03	7½	6.86	9½	8.69
1⅝	1.49	3⅝	3.31	5⅝	5.14	7⅝	6.97	9⅝	8.80
1¾	1.60	3¾	3.43	5¾	5.26	7¾	7.09	9¾	8.92
1⅞	1.71	3⅞	3.54	5⅞	5.37	7⅞	7.20	9⅞	9.03
2	1.83	4	3.66	6	5.49	8	7.32	10	9.14

1.
Easy to Make and Fly

Dart

The Dart is one of the first paper airplanes most people learn to fold. Begin by folding a piece of notebook paper in half the long way. This is shown in Illus. 1. To make sure the fold stays in place, take just a second and crease it. An easy way to do this is to press the back of your thumbnail down firmly and run it along the fold.

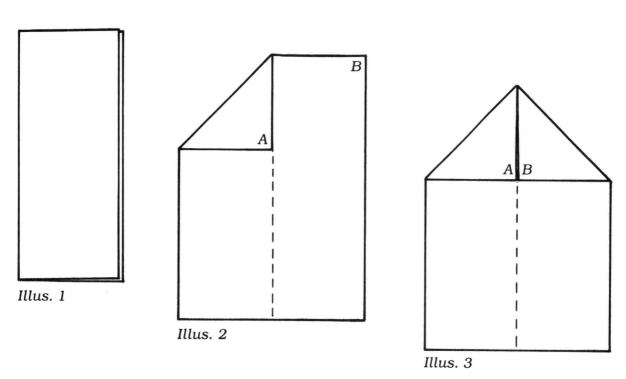

Illus. 1

Illus. 2

Illus. 3

Open the paper back up and fold corner A down to the center line. Crease the fold with your thumbnail so it looks like Illus. 2. For the next step, fold corner B down to the center line as you see in Illus. 3. You have probably already creased this fold with your thumbnail. If not, take a second and do that now.

My thumbnail's getting quite a workout!

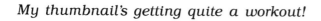

7

When making the Dart or any other paper airplane in this book, don't hurry. Take your time. Make certain you understand each step before you actually take it. Then carefully make your folds. If something does go wrong don't worry. The worst that could happen is that you may have to back up a step or two, and even if you have to start again it's nothing to get upset about.

So far your Dart doesn't look like much, but never fear. It will in a minute. Fold corner C over to the center line and crease the fold. Illus. 4 shows how. Now fold and crease corner D as shown in Illus. 5.

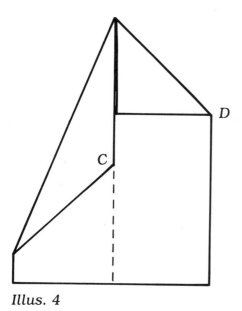

Illus. 4

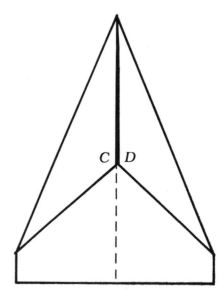

Illus. 5

Turn the paper over and fold side E along the dotted line in Illus. 6. Crease the fold; then unfold side E and crease side F along the dotted line.

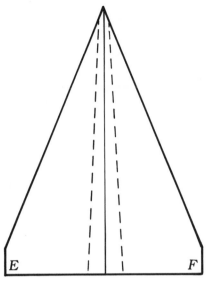

Illus. 6

Unfold side F and turn the Dart over. Grasp the plane's body firmly between your thumb and forefinger. As you do this, the Dart's wings will lift and flatten out.

Now give your Dart its first flight. Hold the plane's body between your thumb and forefinger and give the Dart a quick flick of your wrist. It should fly fast and straight, just like a dart.

After a few flights, try a change in your Dart. Take a short strip of cellophane tape and attach it to each wing as shown in Illus. 7. As you do this, pull up both wings so that when you fasten the ends of the tape you actually lift the outer edges of the wings. Don't try to press the center of the tape down. Now launch the Dart and see how it flies differently than before.

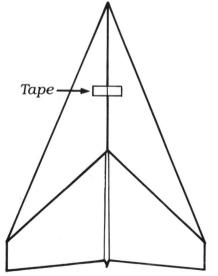

Tape →

Illus. 7

9

Little Dart

Fold corner A of a sheet of notebook paper over to the opposite side of the paper, and crease the fold, so that it looks like Illus. 8. Next, fold corner B over and crease it as in Illus. 9. Now, fold the right side over to the left side, crease this fold, and then unfold Little Dart so that it looks like Illus. 10.

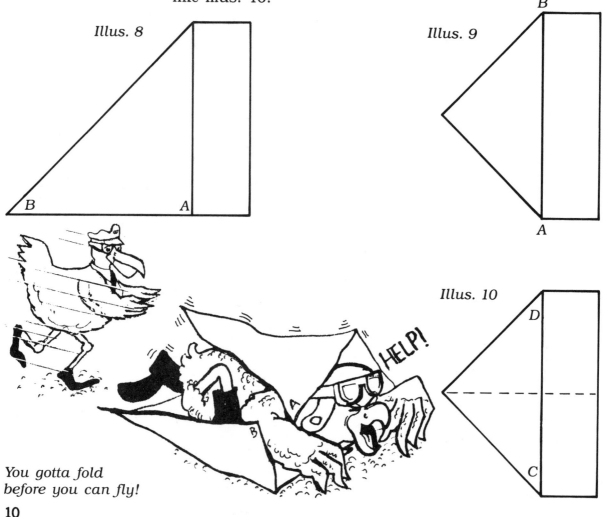

Illus. 8

Illus. 9

Illus. 10

You gotta fold before you can fly!

10

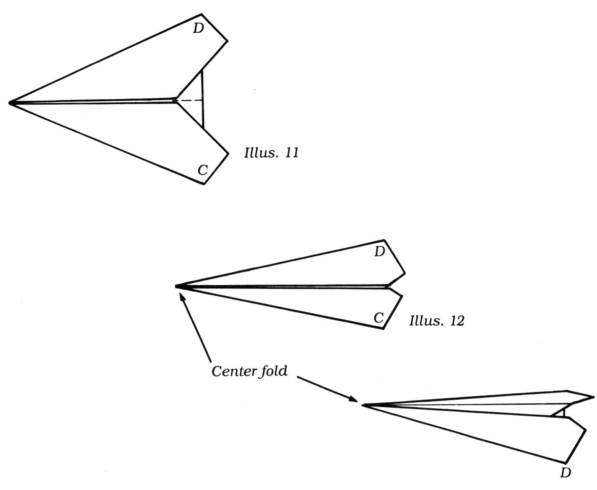

Illus. 11

Illus. 12

Center fold

Illus. 13

Now fold side C over to the center (you're probably creasing each fold without being told by now, so we'll only mention creasing a fold once in a while, just as a reminder); then fold side D to the center as well. Little Dart should look like Illus. 11.

Now fold Little Dart in half along the center fold already in place. Fold side C down to the center so it looks like Illus. 12; then turn Little Dart over and fold side D over the same way. This gives you what you see in Illus. 13.

Let the wings spread when you pick up Little Dart. Take a firm grip on the fuselage and launch Little Dart with a quick flick of the wrist.

After a few flights you may want to use a short piece of cellophane tape to hold the wings together as you did for the Dart. If you decide to tape the wings, remember to pull them up a bit at the outer edges.

From time to time you may want to fly your paper airplanes outdoors. Little Dart should do well outdoors. Just remember to fly paper airplanes safely, whether you're indoors or out.

Little Wonder

The first two airplanes used a rectangular sheet of notebook paper. For Little Wonder you need a square piece of paper. To turn a sheet of notebook paper into a square, fold the top right corner of the paper down to the opposite edge as in Illus. 14; then cut off the paper shown by the slanted lines in Illus. 15. When you unfold the paper you will have a square sheet without any fuss or bother.

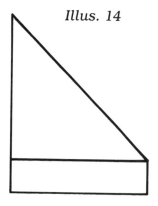

Illus. 14

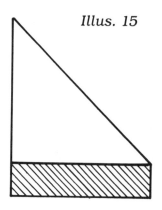

Illus. 15

Fold the paper in half, crease the fold, and unfold it. Now fold side A down to the center line, and unfold this crease as well. The two dotted lines in Illus. 16 show the folds.

Fold corner B up so that it exactly reaches the top fold. Make sure the fold starts at the left end of the center fold—this is very important. Little Wonder should look like Illus. 17.

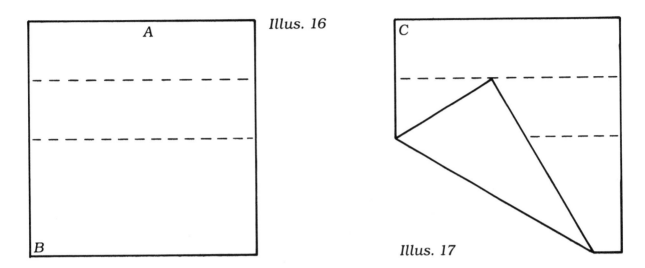

Illus. 16

Illus. 17

Now fold corner C down as you see in Illus. 18. Make sure the fold comes right down over corner B. Next, fold the pointed end D so that the point is exactly even with the center fold at the right hand side of the paper; then unfold it. It should match the dotted line in Illus. 19.

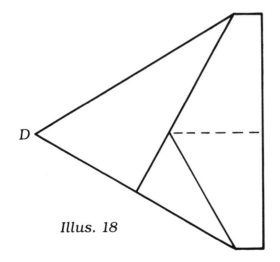

Illus. 18

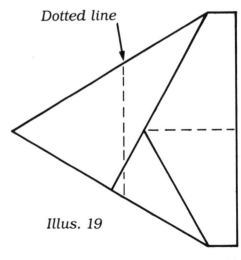

Dotted line

Illus. 19

Now fold point D so that the point touches the crease you made in the last step, and this time don't unfold it. In Illus. 20 you can see this fold and your next fold. Crease the next fold along the dotted line so that the edge of the paper comes right to the crease already in place.

Make one more fold on the plane's nose along the one that is already there, as in Illus. 21. You have quite a bit of paper stacked up now in the plane's nose, but don't worry about this. It's this thick stack of paper that makes Little Wonder fly the way it does.

Next fold

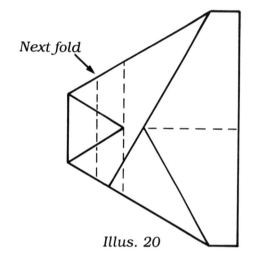

Illus. 20

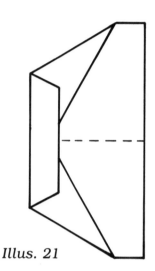

Illus. 21

Fold the wings together along the center fold. Little Wonder is almost ready to fly. The dotted line in Illus. 22 shows where to fold the wings down. Fold the nearest wing down; then turn the plane over and fold the other wing down in the same way. Crease both folds well.

Open the wings and grasp the thick part of the fuselage right behind the nose. Give it a quick toss.

After a few test flights, experiment by launching Little Wonder with a harder throw. Then try an easier toss. Hold

Illus. 22

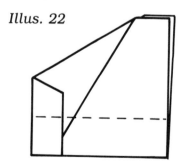

the plane a little farther back from the nose and see what happens.

Now, let's try something completely different. Check Illus. 23 to see how to place your index finger for this launch. That's right! You are going to launch Little Wonder backwards.

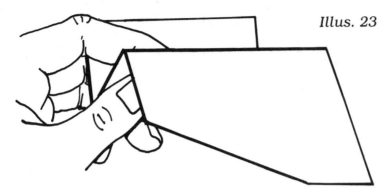

Illus. 23

Lift your hand above your head and snap your hand forward quickly. Release the airplane as your hand comes forward. Little Wonder will do a quick twist in the air so quickly it'll be hard to see. Then it'll fly forward just as airplanes are supposed to fly.

Try this reverse launch a few times until you find out exactly how hard to throw the plane and when to let it slip from your hand. If you need more room to really let Little Wonder do its stuff, try flying it outside. Just remember, don't fly it into the street or among people on the sidewalk. A backyard or playground is just the place.

He said try it backwards!

But not at me!

Easy Glide

The Easy Glide looks very much like Little Wonder. However, as you will see, it flies a lot differently.

Begin with a piece of square paper for Easy Glide. (Remember how to turn a rectangle into a square.) Fold one side of the paper over to the other and crease the fold. Now unfold the paper, as you see in Illus. 24. You should also see two more dotted lines. Fold corners A and B along these lines. When you make these two folds be sure A and B come exactly to the center fold, so that your Easy Glide looks like Illus. 25.

Next, fold the nose of the airplane back to the tail, crease it, and unfold it. You can see this fold in Illus. 26, as well as a dotted line showing the next fold. Fold the nose over so

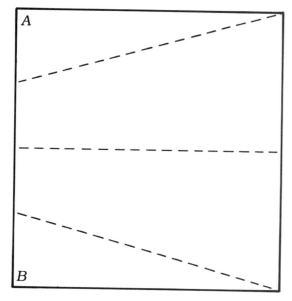

Illus. 24

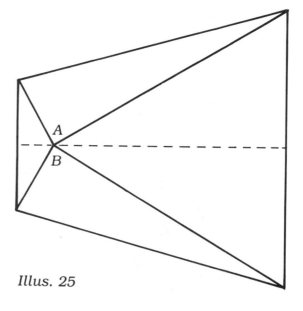

Illus. 25

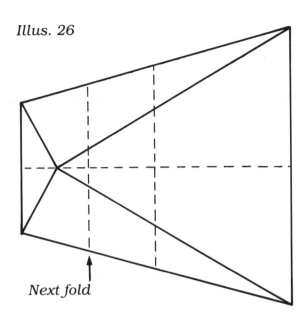

Next fold

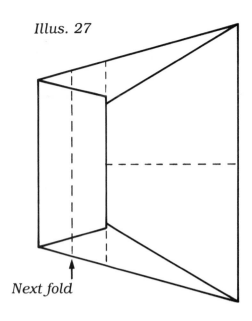

Next fold

that it just touches the fold you just made a few seconds ago, so your plane looks like Illus. 27. Now fold the nose again along the dotted line in Illus. 27; then fold the nose one more time along the crease you have been using as a guide. Your Easy Glide should look like Illus. 28.

Fold your airplane in half along the center line in Illus. 28. Now fold the wings down, using the dotted line in Illus. 29 as a guide. Note that the fuselage of Easy Glide is not quite as high as Little Wonder's. Fold and crease the front wing down along the dotted line first; then turn Easy Glide

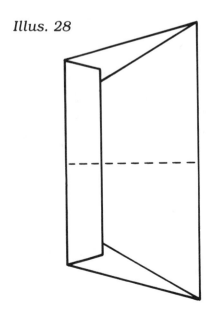

Illus. 28

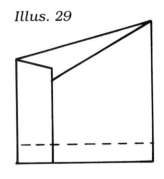

Illus. 29

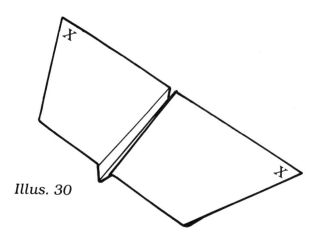

Illus. 30

over and fold down the second wing. Lift the wings into place and Easy Glide appears as seen in Illus. 30. Note the two X's on the rear corners of the wings. We will get to them in just a minute.

Launch Easy Glide with a smooth movement of your hand. Don't toss it hard, just let it glide out of your hand. If it glides nicely, you're a fantastic paper-airplane builder. If it crashes, you are about to become a fantastic airplane builder.

Let's assume the worst and figure that your Easy Glide crashed shortly after launching. Now we will do some experiments to see what we can do to make it glide correctly. First, try launching it a little harder.

Did it still stall? Here's where the little X's on the wings come in. Gently bend (don't fold!) the wings up so that the corners of the wings where the X's are turn upwards slightly. An easy way to do this is to put your thumb on the top of a wing and your fingers beneath the wing. Just pull your hand backwards and upwards along the wing, letting your thumb and fingers bend it.

Now make another test flight. Easy Glide should do a bit better now. If it is still stalling or fluttering down after just a few feet, don't give up hope. Put a paper clip onto the nose part of the fuselage; making sure the clip holds both sides of the fuselage together. Now give Easy Glide a smooth launch. It should fly with an easy gliding motion.

Stall When any airplane seems to stop in midair and then fall or flutter to the ground, it stalls. Pilots have a stall warning in their airliners to warn them before a stall occurs. With paper airplanes we just have to test fly them.

Flight Characteristics The way in which an airplane flies depends upon its flight characteristics. A plane's characteristics could be long and straight, short and looping, fast or slow.

Playground Favorite

This airplane is called the Playground Favorite because it has been flown by children on school playgrounds for years and years. Some airplanes got to be popular because they were easy to make and flew well, and this is one of them.

Begin with a rectangular piece of notebook paper. Fold it lengthwise in the center to get a center crease; then unfold the paper. Now, fold corner A making certain the fold begins right at the center line. Fold corner B over the same way, so your plane looks like Illus. 31.

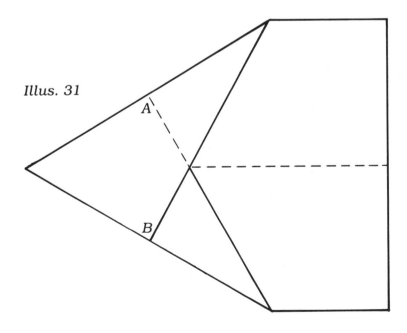

Illus. 31

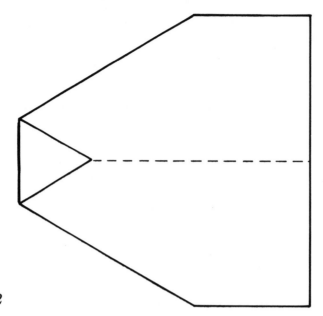

Illus. 32

Turn your Playground Favorite over, and fold the nose back about two inches, as you can see in Illus. 32. Now fold the airplane upwards along the center fold. Look at the dotted line in Illus. 33 to see where to fold the wings down.

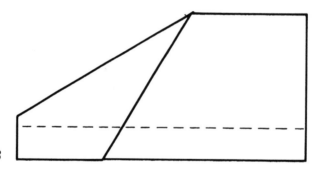

Illus. 33

Fold the wing nearest you down and crease it into place; then turn Playground Favorite over and fold down the other wing. Now, take a good look at the dotted line shown in Illus. 34. This is where you will be making a second wing fold.

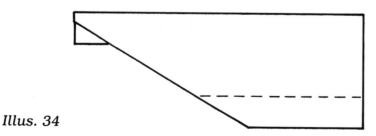

Illus. 34

Fold the wing nearest you up along the dotted line; then turn the airplane over and fold the other wing. Straighten the wings upwards and launch your Playground Favorite with a quick snap of your arm and wrist. Within a few flights you'll begin to get the feel of exactly how hard you need to launch this airplane to get the best flight.

Just as an experiment, slip a paper clip onto the airplane's nose. Again test it with different launch speeds. You may want to continue flying the plane with the paper clip in place or you may decide to remove it. This all depends upon the weight of the paper you used, air currents, and exactly how your wings are folded.

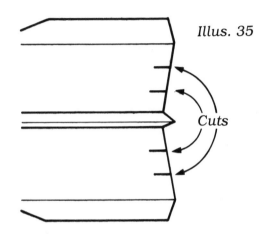

Illus. 35

Cuts

After you have made several successful flights, it's time to do some research. With a pair of scissors, make the four cuts shown in Illus. 35. Now bend the paper between each pair of cuts upwards and give Playground Favorite a test flight.

Try another launch with a bit more speed. With both flaps up, your airplane will either make a loop in the air or will start into a loop and then turn and fly back towards you. Experiment: bend the flaps straight up; then just partway up. It is amazing how these small flaps will change the way your airplane performs. Try it with both flaps down, first all the way down, then part of the way down; then bend one flap up and the other down. See what happens when one flap is straight up and the other only part of the way down.

From now on you will probably want to experiment with the paper airplanes you construct. Think about folding the wings a little differently than the way they are first folded. Consider making control flaps of different sizes. Try making them very narrow. See how small you can make flaps which will still change the way your airplane flies.

PILOT'S CORNER

Control Surfaces Flaps such as the ones on Playground Favorite are called control surfaces. This is because of the way they control or change an airplane's flight.

Stabilizers Stabilizers help keep an airplane steady in flight. Most airplanes use only one stabilizer located on the center of the fuselage. The moveable flap at the rear of the vertical stabilizer is called the rudder. Pilot's use the rudder to turn while in flight. Since your stabilizers can move, you may call them rudders and be correct.

Little Stubby

The first step in folding Little Stubby is to begin with a square piece of paper, like we did with Little Wonder. Fold corner A in Illus. 36 over to the opposite corner, crease it; then unfold the paper. Now fold corner B in the same way over to its opposite corner and unfold it.

Make the fold shown by the smallest dotted line in Illus. 36 by folding corner A to the exact center of the sheet of paper. Don't unfold it this time. Look at Illus. 37. You'll see

Illus. 36

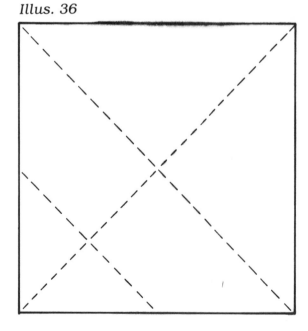

Illus. 37

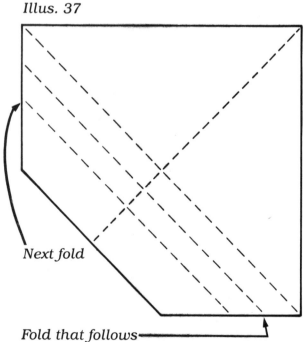

Next fold

Fold that follows

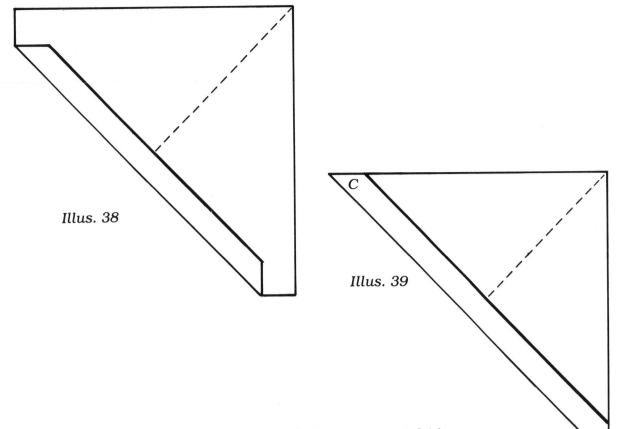

Illus. 38

Illus. 39

how the plane looks at this point, and also your next fold. Make this fold; then check the next dotted line which indicates the fold that follows. As you can see in Illus. 38, these folds should bring the airplane's nose folds right up to the center fold we made at the very beginning of construction.

Make one more fold by creasing the nose section right over. Illus. 39 shows how Little Stubby looks now.

Turn the paper over and fold corner C to the opposite corner. Make sure your airplane looks like Illus. 40. The dotted line shows where to fold back corner D. Make sure it goes back to the tip of the tail; then crease it well. Turn the paper over and make the same fold with corner C. What you have now is the triangular piece of paper in Illus. 41.

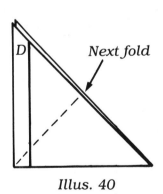

Next fold

Illus. 40

Illus. 41

Nose flap

23

Look at the little nose flap shown by the arrow. Pull this nose flap down and forward so that it forms a square nose for Little Stubby. As you pull down and forward on the nose flap, the plane's wings will open up. This is supposed to happen, so don't panic when Little Stubby seems to begin to spread apart in your hands. As the wings open, the fuselage will also spread out a bit. When the nose flap is pulled into place your Little Stubby should look like Illus. 42.

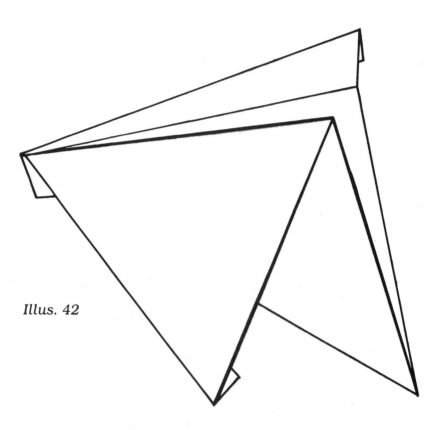

Illus. 42

Hold Little Stubby by its fuselage just behind the nose flap, and give it a gentle push to send it into the air. Remember, we said gentle! Little Stubby is one of those airplanes which does not like to be launched at high speed.

Just for an experiment, try launching your Little Stubby with a hard push to see what happens.

You may also try adjusting the nose flap either upward, or downward, a bit to see how this affects the way Little Stubby flies. When the nose flap moves you will see the wings move as well. Try a paper clip on its nose to see how this will affect flights. Whatever you try, Little Stubby will be good for short, easy flights.

School Yard Special

Paper airplanes of this type have had a way of showing up on school yards for years and years. Some people say they fly out of school windows, but of course you and I don't know anything about that.

Do you know who flew that plane?

I dunno anything!

25

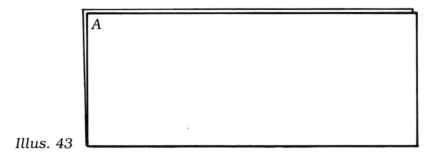

Illus. 43

Start with a sheet of notebook paper. Fold it in half the long way and leave it folded, so it looks like Illus. 43. Fold corner A down and crease it into place. Turn the airplane over and fold down the other front corner as well. Now turn the airplane back over and make the next fold in Illus. 44. Fold the wing nearest you down and crease it along the dotted line; then turn the airplane over and do the same for the other wing, so that your School Yard Special looks like Illus. 45.

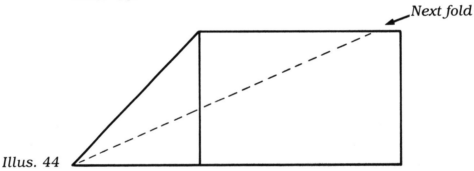

Next fold

Illus. 44

Look at the dotted line in Illus. 45. Before you make this fold, note that the dotted line runs from the point of the nose. In other words this fold is a slanting fold. It is not like the wing folds we have made for most of our paper airplanes thus far. Now that you are aware this fold comes

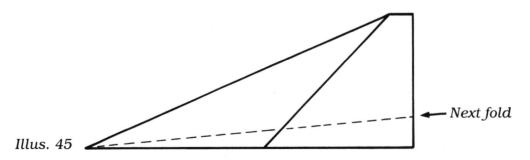

Illus. 45 *Next fold*

back at an angle from the nose, fold both wings down; then straighten the wings back up so that the School Yard Special looks like Illus. 46. The wing fold is now shown. Use a piece of cellophane tape or a staple to fasten the loose edges together at the bottom of the fuselage. Now cut the slit shown in Illus. 46 in each wing.

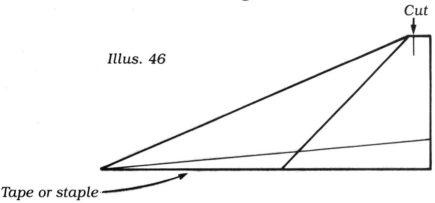

Illus. 46

Cut

Tape or staple

Flatten the wings into place; then fold up the two pieces you made with the two cuts. Once these two parts are standing up they become a pair of vertical stabilizers. Your finished airplane should look very much like the one shown in Illus. 47.

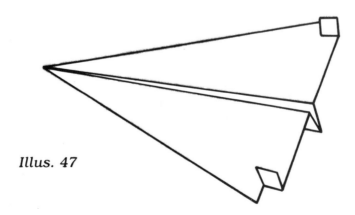

Illus. 47

Take your newest model for a few test flights. It should do a nice job of gliding in a fairly smooth path.

After you have flown the School Yard Special a few times you may want to modify it just a bit. Remember when we made the Dart how we used a small strip of cellophane tape to lift the edges of its wings? As an experiment, you may want to do the same thing with this airplane. The reason for using a piece of tape is to lift the outer edges of the wings.

PILOT'S CORNER

Dihedral The lift of the wing tips or outer edges is known as dihedral. In Illus. 48 you see the front view of an airplane. The dihedral for its wings is easy to see.

Illus. 48

Bulldog

An English Bulldog is the dog with the thick shoulders and heavy head whose nose looks all mashed in as though it has run into a door. After you finish folding the Bulldog, you'll be able to see why it has this name.

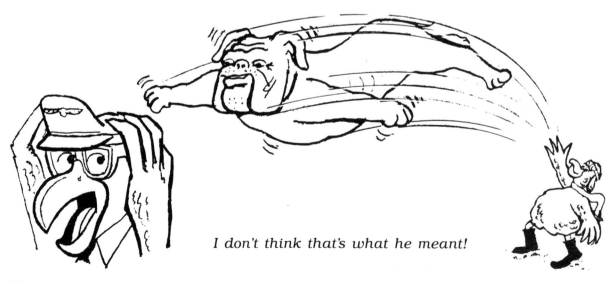

I don't think that's what he meant!

28

Begin with a piece of notebook paper. Fold corner A over to the opposite side, so that it looks like Illus. 49. Then unfold the paper.

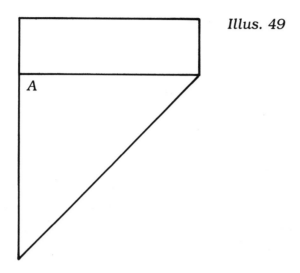

Illus. 49

Next, fold corner B over to its opposite corner, crease it, and (you guessed it) unfold it. At this point the Bulldog-to-be looks like Illus. 50.

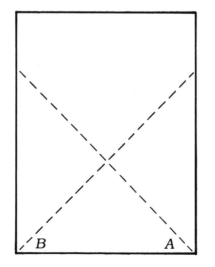

Illus. 50

Now turn the paper over. Fold corners A and B up, so that they meet the creases at the top of the paper. If your creases look like Illus. 51, you've done it right.

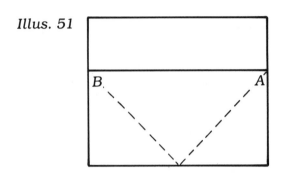

Illus. 51

Now open the paper flat and turn it over again. The folds in your Bulldog look like Illus. 52. Hold the paper firmly at the two points shown by the arrows in Illus. 52.

Now comes the tricky part! Slowly and firmly, push in with both hands. Don't get in a hurry and don't try to bully the paper. If you get rough, the paper will not cooperate and your Bulldog will never get built.

As your hands push the paper together, the bottom corners A and B will lift up, and when the two arrows come together the Bulldog should look like Illus. 53. Note the position of corners A and B.

Illus. 52

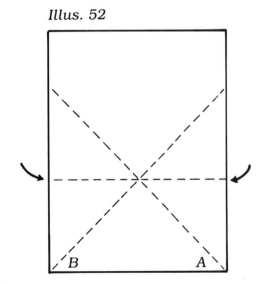

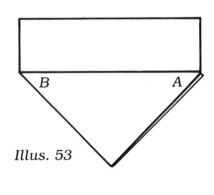

Illus. 53

What has happened is that you have sort of turned part of the Bulldog inside out. You may feel as though you need two pairs of hands, but don't give up; this is the only difficult part of the Bulldog.

Fold corner A down and crease it into place, folding down only the first two layers of paper which you just pulled up. Next, fold down corner B in the same way. If your Bulldog looks like Illus. 54, you are in fine shape. Fold the nose back and crease it firmly.

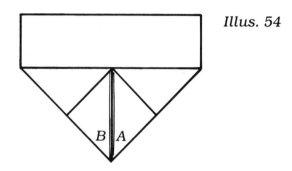

Illus. 54

Fold the paper in half so that it looks like Illus. 55. Then make the next fold, shown by the dotted line.

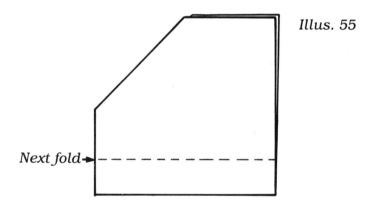

Illus. 55

Next fold→

Fold the wing nearest you down, crease that fold; then turn the Bulldog over. Fold the other wing down so it matches the first wing. Spread the Bulldog's wings open and it's ready for its first test flight.

There won't be any need of a paper clip to give the Bulldog enough weight in its nose; so just launch it with a quick snap of the wrist. It should take off and fly nicely.

Remember when we launched the Little Wonder backwards? Try holding Bulldog the same way and launching it backwards. You should get a good flight.

After you fly this airplane a few times, try some experimental changes to see how they change the way it flies.

Fold the outer edges of the wings upwards along the dotted lines in Illus. 56. Now test-fly the Bulldog and see how it does.

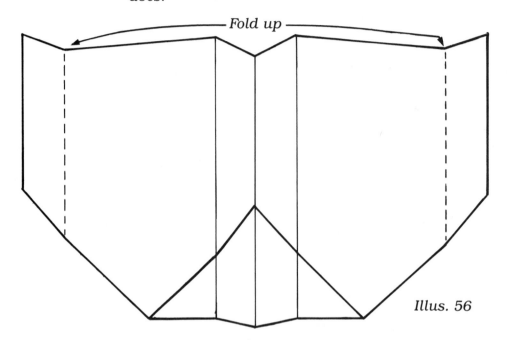

Illus. 56

Try this idea. Fold the outer edges of the wings down. You will see a little different sort of flight pattern than before.

Fold one wing edge down and the other up. This will give you an entirely different kind of flight than the ones you have just experienced.

Try making another Bulldog; this time folding the wings so the fuselage is higher than your first model. Then make one in which the fuselage is a bit lower than your first design. Make a model in which the outer wing edges are extremely narrow. Make another in which these outer edges are quite wide.

The great thing about experimenting with paper airplanes is that you can't really do anything terribly wrong. The absolute worst that can happen is that it won't fly, and should that happen you can examine the design and probably figure out what you did to make the airplane unairworthy (a great word which means the aircraft can't fly properly).

Most of the fun from folding and flying paper airplanes comes from experimenting with changes in design. Feel free to do some design research on each and every model you make.

Remember, there is no such thing as a best paper airplane, neither is there a worst model. The only way to tell how a change will affect the way a model flies is to make that change. If something does not work out, don't do it again. Keep in mind an experimental change that helps the way your model flies.

PILOT'S CORNER

Trim When we adjust the trim of an airplane, it's not the sort of trimming we do with scissors. It's more like balancing the airplane so that it flies properly.

Adding paper clips to the nose is one way of adjusting the trim. Shaping the wings is another way. Check the trim when your airplanes don't fly properly the first time.

2.
Different Folds
for
Different Planes

In this chapter we will be folding paper airplanes that are just a bit different than those we did before. Some of them look quite different, while others look a lot like airplanes we have already folded but fly differently.

Looper

You'll need a pair of scissors for Looper, but other than that all it requires is a sheet of notebook paper and a few quick folds.

Begin the Looper by folding the right-hand side of your paper over about ¼ inch, as in Illus. 57. Fold the paper over and over (you can roll the paper one fold at a time but be sure to crease each fold into place), along the dotted lines in Illus. 58. Keep folding until you get halfway across the paper. You should have about 4½ inches left unfolded. Now fold the paper in half and leave it folded, so that your Looper looks like Illus. 59.

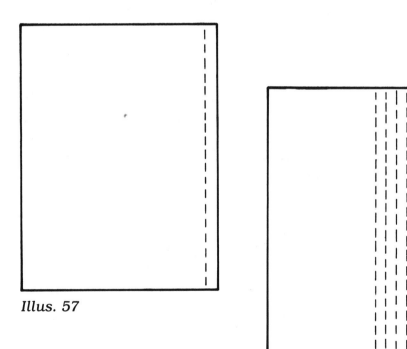

Illus. 57

Illus. 58

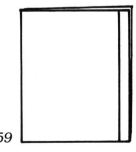

Illus. 59

Here is where the scissors come in. Cut along the dotted line seen in Illus. 60. Hold the Looper firmly while making this cut since you are cutting through two thicknesses of paper and you want both sides of the Looper to be exactly the same. When you're done your Looper should look like Illus. 61. Be sure to take just a second to toss the two scraps into the wastebasket. It's one thing to be a creative paper airplane folder; it's another to be a messy one!

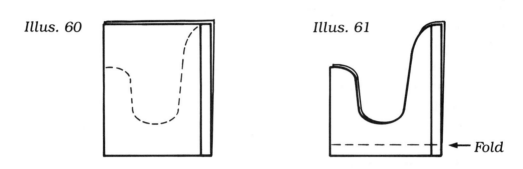

Illus. 60

Illus. 61

← *Fold*

In Illus. 61 you will also see where to fold down the wings. The fuselage will be very narrow. Fold the wing nearest you and crease it; then turn the Looper over and fold the other wing. At this point your Looper is seen in Illus. 62.

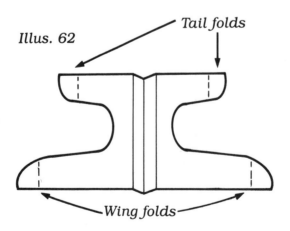

Tail folds

Illus. 62

Wing folds

You may have already realized the dotted lines in Illus. 62 indicate folds. But wait—not all the folds are the same: fold the wing tips up; then fold the ends of the tail down. When the folding is done the Looper is ready to fly. It should look like Illus. 63.

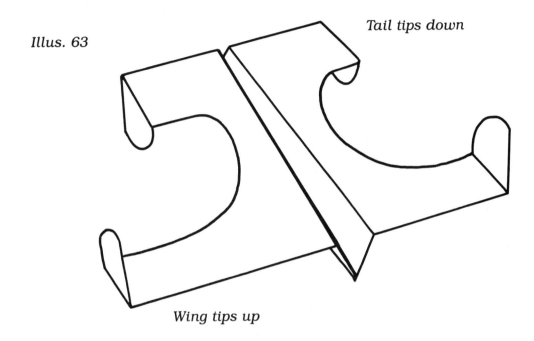

Illus. 63

Tail tips down

Wing tips up

Test the Looper with a couple of quick flights. Try launching it backwards like you did with Little Wonder; then, take the Looper into either a very large room or outdoors and launch it with a good, quick snap of your hand and wrist.

After a few flights try launching the Looper almost straight up; then at a little less of an angle. With just a little research you will discover how best to launch the Looper so that it will do at least one loop for you.

The Looper is such a great little airplane you may want to make another one and try cutting its wings and tail a little differently than your first model. Make the wings a little wider or narrower; or change the wing and tail folds so that the tips are different from your first model.

PILOT'S CORNER

Ailerons Very early in aviation history the people building airplanes discovered that a wing with a curved upper surface provided more lift than did a flat wing. This is because air passing over the curved wing's surface moves faster. The faster the air moves, the lower the air pressure. Low air pressure on top of an airplane's wings gives that airplane more lift.

It was not long before special control surfaces were added to airplane wings, called ailerons. (So far we have called them flaps.) Ailerons are on the back of an airplane's wings. Moving them up or down changes the shape of the wing. By making the wing either more or less curved the pilot controls the amount of lift the wing gives the airplane.

On take off the airplane needs a lot of lift to get off the ground. Therefore, the ailerons are set so that their rear edges point downwards. This gives the top of the wing more curve. Illus. 64 gives you an idea of how a wing looks with the ailerons down.

Illus. 64

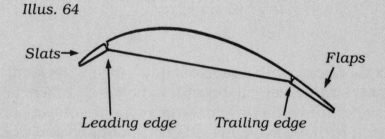

Slats→   Flaps

Leading edge   *Trailing edge*

Leading Edge, Trailing Edge The front of the wing is the leading edge. This is logical since the front leads. The rear of the wing is the trailing edge, since it follows behind.

Tjaden Twister

This plane is named after its builder, Bryon Tjaden, a student at Brentwood Middle School in Greeley, Colorado. You will discover for yourself why it is called Twister after you make your first test flight.

Fold a sheet of notebook paper down the middle and then unfold it. Illus. 65 shows these folds as corners A and B.

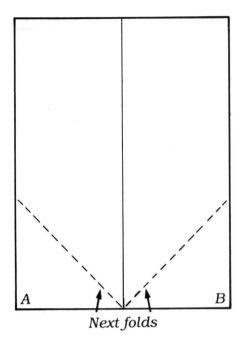

Illus. 65

Next folds

Fold both corners in to the center and crease the folds. The next folds are in Illus. 66. When you make these two folds, be sure both sides of the paper come all the way to the center fold.

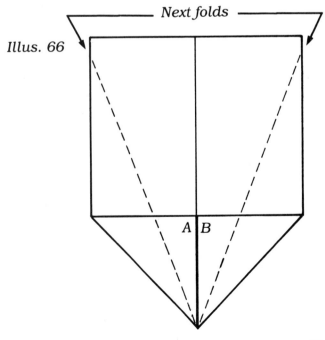

Illus. 66

Next folds

Fold the airplane along its original center fold so that it looks like Illus. 67. You'll also see a dotted line that shows you the wing folds.

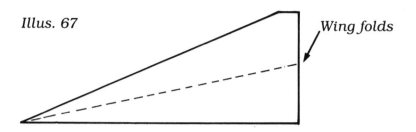

Illus. 67   *Wing folds*

Fold the wing nearest to you along the dotted line as shown in Illus. 67. Be sure the edge of the wing comes right down to the center fold. Now turn the Twister over and fold down the second wing in the same manner. Your Twister should look like Illus. 68.

Illus. 68

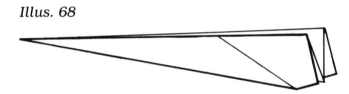

Grasp the fuselage and lift the wings into flying position, but don't launch it yet. Look at Illus. 69. Fold corner C down along the dotted line shown in Illus. 69. Then fold corner D up in the same manner. These folded corners will be extremely important control surfaces for your airplane, because they will make the plane twist as it flies. Now give your Tjaden Twister its first launch.

Illus. 69   *Corner D*

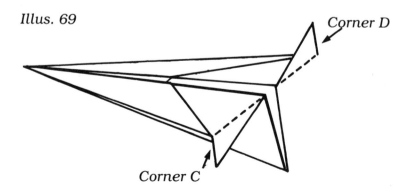

Corner C

Do a little research by making those folded corners smaller and then larger than your original folds. What does this do to the airplane's speed and distance?

For one final research project reverse the folds and fold corner C up while corner D is folded down. You can probably predict what will happen to the way your latest airplane flies. Launch it with these changes and see if it behaves the way you thought it would.

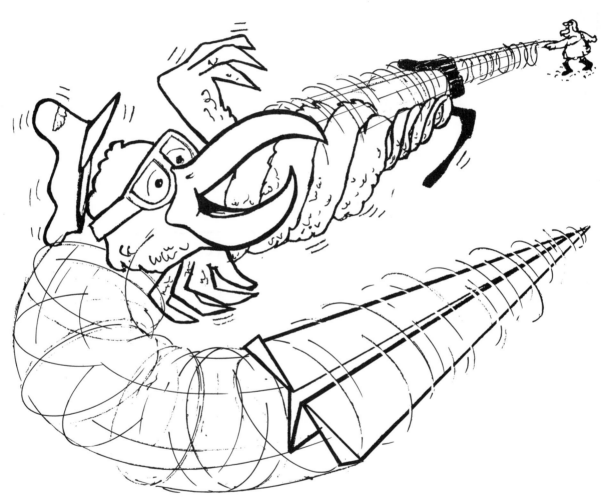

I didn't think it would do that!

PILOT'S CORNER

Horizontal Stabilizer; Vertical Stabilizer The horizontal stabilizer, in case you didn't already know, is part of the tail section. The other part is the vertical stabilizer.

Spinner

Begin Spinner with a sheet of notebook paper. Cut off about 1½ inches along one side. This is the shaded area in Illus. 70.

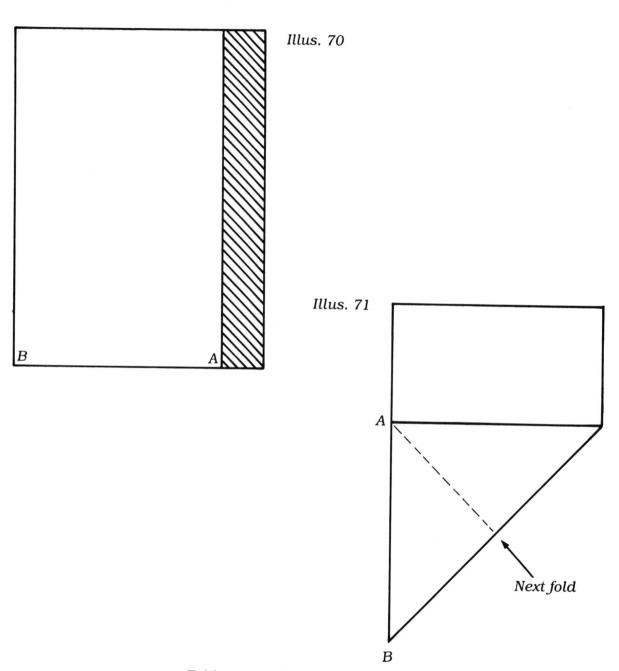

Illus. 70

Illus. 71

Next fold

Fold corner A over and crease it into place as shown in Illus. 71; then fold corner B over in the same way. (Follow the dotted line in Illus. 71.)

Now unfold the paper so it lies flat. Fold the bottom edge up along the dotted line at the arrows in Illus. 72. When you make the fold the creases from the bottom edge should exactly match the creases toward the middle of the paper.

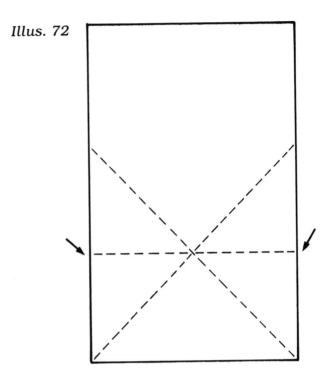

Illus. 72

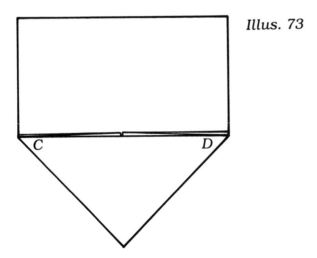

Illus. 73

Now, put your hands at either end of the fold you just made (if you need help, look back at the arrows in Illus. 72) and push the paper in lightly. If you have folded it right, it should look like Illus. 73.

Fold corners C and D down to the nose point. Illus. 74 shows how Spinner looks at this stage.

Turn the airplane over and fold the nose back as seen in Illus. 75. Fold back only the double thickness of paper on the top after you turn the airplane over. Leave two points of paper still unfolded. These points are corners C and D which you folded down just a minute ago.

Illus. 74

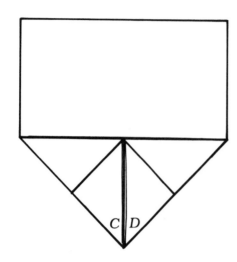

Illus. 75

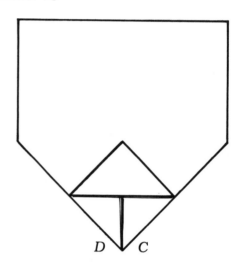

Now fold the Spinner in half down its center, and look at Illus. 76. You see how your plane looks after the folds, and also where to cut. With your scissors, cut along the dotted line (remember to throw away the scrap). Nose points C and D are now on the outside of the fold.

Illus. 76

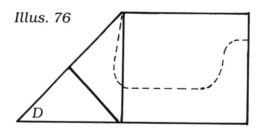

When you cut, be sure to hold the two sides of the airplane firmly so they do not slip. The cuttings may be just a little harder when you cut the rest of the wings, because you are cutting through four layers of paper.

After the scissor work is finished the Spinner will look like Illus. 77. The dotted lines show where to fold down the wings and the tail. You can staple the nose if you have a stapler handy. If not, use a piece of tape to hold the two nose points together.

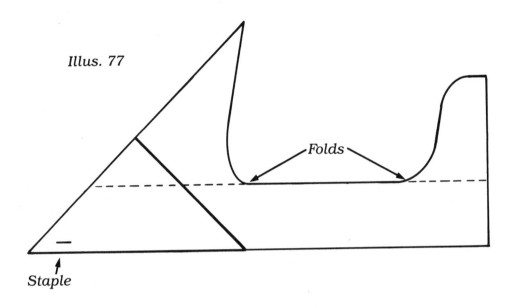

Illus. 77

Folds

Staple

Launch Spinner with a quick snap of the wrist. With its thick nose folds you shouldn't need a paper clip.

Spinner is a good outdoor airplane. If everything goes well you should be able to get Spinner to do a loop once in a while as well as spin while in flight.

If you want to experiment make another Spinner airplane in which you change the shape of the trailing edge of the wings. (If you forgot about trailing edges, just look at page 40.) Perhaps you would like to change the size and shape of the tail. Just for fun, cut out a vertical stabilizer and glue it into place between the two horizontal stabilizers in Spinner's tail, but when you see it fly with it you may want to change Spinner's name.

Loop and Turn

The minute you saw the name of this paper airplane you probably had a pretty good idea what to expect from it when it flies. If all goes well you won't be disappointed.

Begin by folding a sheet of notebook paper in half. Fold the lower-left hand corner over and crease it into place. Make sure the bottom edge of the fold extends just a bit past the center line. You'll see the reason for this in a minute. Illus. 78 shows how your airplane looks at this point.

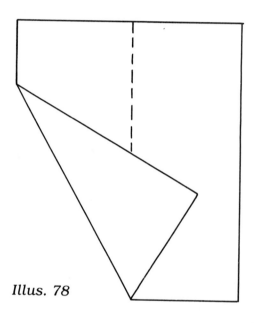

Illus. 78

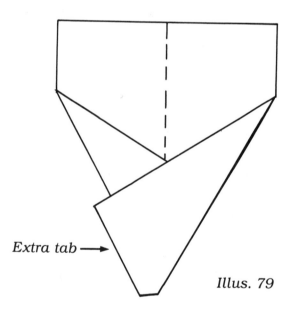

Extra tab →

Illus. 79

Fold the opposite side as shown in Illus. 79. Make absolutely certain that the upper end of the fold is exactly even with the top of the other fold. The two arrows in Illus. 79 show these two locations. You'll have a tab of paper hanging over the edge of the nose, but don't worry, we'll take care of that. Illus. 80 shows how. Fold the tab around and

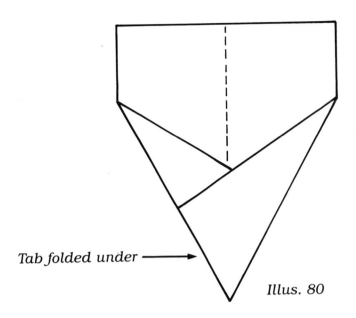

Tab folded under ⟶

Illus. 80

under the airplane and crease the fold into place. You may have figured out that the tab is there to lock the first two folds into place. Remember that the first fold extended a bit past the center line.

Turn your paper airplane over so that the side with the tab now faces up. Fold about 3 inches of the nose back so your plane looks like Illus. 81.

Illus. 81

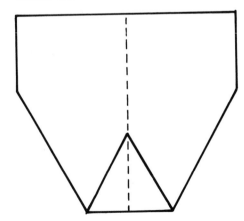

Now fold your Loop and Turn in half. Make sure the nose fold is on the inside. The dotted line in Illus. 82 shows where you will make the wing folds. Fold the wing closest to you down along that dotted line and crease it into place; then turn the airplane over and fold down the other wing.

Illus. 83 is a side view of your plane. The dotted line tells you where to fold the wing edge.

Illus. 82

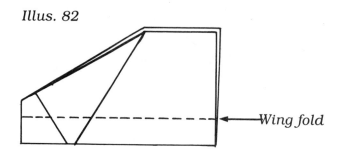

Wing fold

Illus. 83

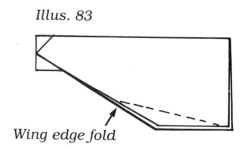

Wing edge fold

Take a careful look at the fold before you make it. Note that the fold runs at an angle from front to back. When the fold reaches the tail section it's at the very corner of the paper.

Now fold the wing nearest you up along this dotted line; then turn the airplane over and fold the other wing edge up as well. Make sure that you fold the edges up, not down.

Unfold the Loop and Turn so that it looks about like Illus. 84.

Use scissors to cut the slits for the two flaps in the trailing edge of the wing. Then fold both flaps up.

Your airplane is ready for its first test flight.

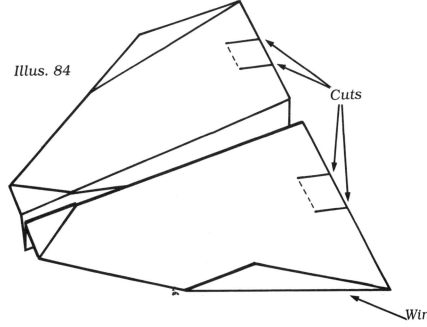

Illus. 84

Cuts

Wing edges up

Launch Loop and Turn firmly but don't give it too much thrust. It should make a loop and then turn to glide to a landing. This airplane should do a good job of flying outside if there's not too much breeze.

For some experimental flights try these ideas. See what happens when the control flaps are not extended up completely. Fly the airplane with the flaps halfway up, a fourth of the way up, and all the way up. Then try it with one of the control flaps down and the other one up.

Fold both flaps back in the up position, then the wing edges down rather than up to see how that affects the flight. Try one wing edge up and the other down.

With all this experimental research you should have a pretty good idea how certain changes will affect your paper airplanes.

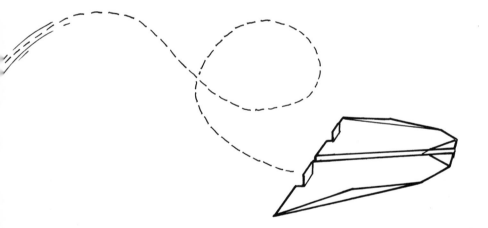

3.
Cut,
Glue,
and Fly

The paper airplanes in this chapter are a bit different from those we have been flying. Since these airplanes are cut out, then glued or stapled together, you'll need scissors and either glue or a stapler. White school glue is perfect, but rubber cement, paste or another sort of glue will work just fine.

You'll also need paper which is a little stiffer than regular notebook paper for these airplanes. The big brown grocery bags you get at the supermarket do a good job, as does any other paper which is a bit heavier and stiffer than notebook paper. Manila folders can be used to construct some of these airplanes, but if you use something this heavy you may have a bit more trouble trimming some of the airplanes.

You'll also need a pencil and a ruler because you have to draw these airplanes before cutting them out. Don't worry if you are not a great artist—the plans are easy to follow.

It's a good thing the plans are easy!

PILOT'S CORNER

Trimming Tips You know by now that placing paper clips at the nose will give a stalling airplane more weight forward, so that it has proper balance.

Sometimes it's better to move the paper clip back an inch or more from the nose. This is one of those things you discover only through trial and error during test flights, so don't be afraid to experiment. If you move a paper clip too far and the airplane crashes, no harm done. Just change the clip's location and take another test flight.

When you fly your paper airplanes outdoors you'll find that you usually must launch airplanes faster because the air movements are stronger.

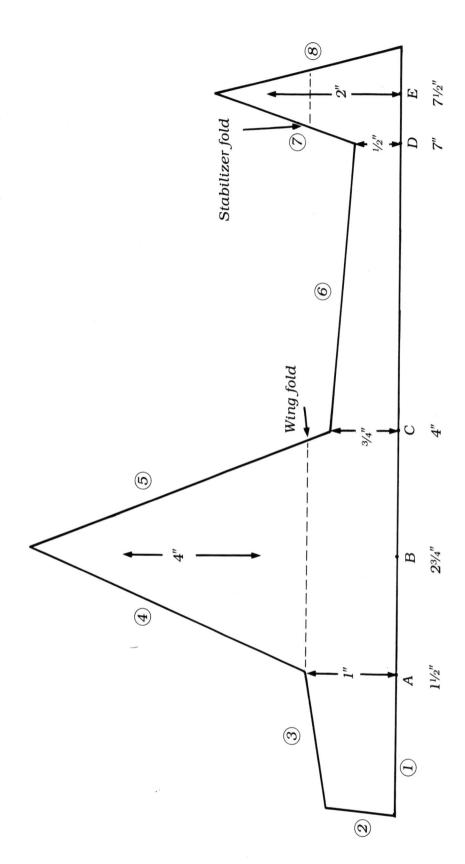

56

Illus. 85

Spike

In Illus. 85 you see only half of Spike. This is because you will be cutting this and the other airplanes in this chapter from a folded piece of material. If this doesn't make sense to you don't worry, it will when it's time to cut. When you draw the plans for Spike, don't worry if your drawing is a fraction of an inch different from Illus. 85. in the book. Your airplane should fly even if it is not exactly like the original. That's the great thing about paper airplanes—if something goes a little bit wrong the airplane will still almost always fly.

Begin by drawing an 8-inch straight line. Make sure you leave at least 4 inches of your paper on either side of this line, so that when you fold along this line before cutting you have enough room to cut out both sides of the airplane. Mark this line number 1 (as in Illus. 00). All the line numbers are circled in Illus. 85 so you can find them easily.

Now locate the five dots on line 1. Measure all the dots from the left side of the line. Dot A is 1½ inches from the left side; dot B is 2¾ inches; dot C is 4 inches from the left side. Dot D is 7 inches from the left end; and finally dot E is 7½ inches from the beginning of the line.

Make line 2 ¾ inch in length and be sure that it slants back just a bit. This will be Spike's nose.

Measure up from dot A one inch, and mark that point. Then draw line 3 to connect the upper end of line with this dot.

Next, measure up 4 inches from dot B, and mark that point. Connect this dot with line 3 to make line 4.

Measure ¾ inch up from dot C, and connect the end of line 4 with this point. This will make line 5.

From dot D measure upwards ½ inch. Connect this point with the end of line 5 to put line 6 in place.

Don't give up now. Spike is almost ready to cut out.

Measure upwards from dot E 2 inches. Draw line 7 from this point to the end of line 6. Then finish Spike's outline by connecting the end of line 7 with the end of the long line.

Now fold your stiff paper along the long line, so that you'll have a double thickness of material. When you cut out the pattern you will be cutting through two sheets. Hold the material together very, very carefully, and don't let the bottom layer slip. If you do, Spike will come out lopsided and we don't want that.

First you fold, then you fly!

When the airplane is cut out, fold the wings and horizontal stabilizer into place. Fold the wing nearest to you along the dotted line in Illus. 85; then fold the other wing in the same manner, and do the same for the horizontal stabilizer. Since the horizontal stabilizer is so high up, all the rest of the material acts as the vertical stabilizer.

Spread glue on the inside of the fuselage and let it dry. You can hold the fuselage together with several paper clips while the glue dries. Or, you can straighten the wings and stabilizer and press Spike under a book. If you do it this way just don't let any glue spread onto the wings or stabilizer, or it'll spread onto your book!

When the glue dries (and it only takes a minute or two) it is time for Spike's test flight.

You will probably need a paper clip on this airplane's nose to trim it properly. Just remember that if the airplane starts to roll or pitch, it needs a bit more nose weight. If it immediately dives to the ground, its nose is too heavy.

There are two things you can do if you want to make Spike stronger. You can also use these on any of the cut and glue planes.

First, you can make a wing brace. A wing brace is glued onto the top of the wings. In Illus. 86 you can see Spike's wings with a wing brace in place. This brace is the same shape as the airplane's wings. If you don't want to be that fancy, a square or rectangular strip of material (or even a triangle) works just as well.

Illus. 86

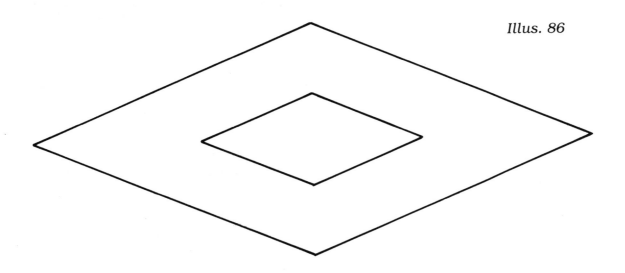

The second thing you can do to strengthen one of these airplanes is to put a little strip of tape beneath each side of the horizontal stabilizer. Illus. 87 shows how to do this.

Illus. 87

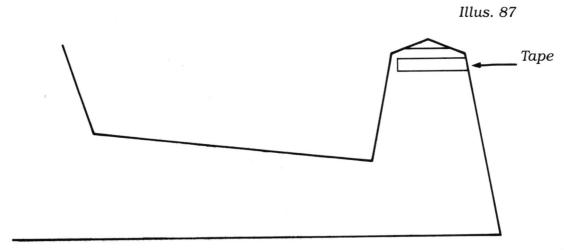

Tape

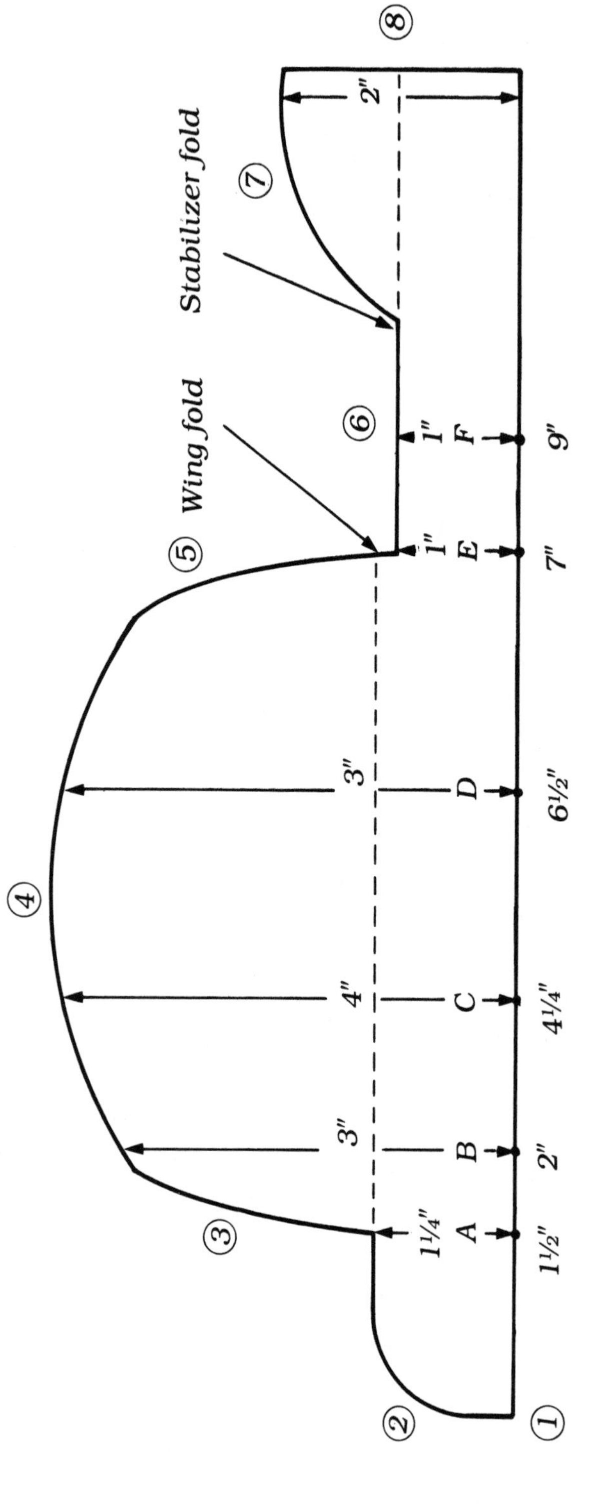

Cruiser

You'll need a pencil compass for Cruiser's wings and tail assembly, but if you don't have one, don't worry. You can use anything flat and round, such as a can or a lid from a cooking pan instead of the compass. A one-pound coffee can makes a great 4-inch circle, which you'll need for both the vertical and horizontal stabilizers. An 8-inch lid from a pot or pan is just fine for drawing Cruiser's round wing tips.

Of course, if you don't have a compass or the right-sized can or pan lid, draw the curves freehand. As we said before, the wonderful thing about most of these paper airplanes is they will fly even if they are not made exactly according to plans.

Draw line 1 11 inches long as in Illus. 88. Remember to draw line 1 at least 4 inches from the side of your material, so that you can fold the material double along this long line before cutting out the Cruiser.

The next step is to locate and mark the dots along line 1. Dot A is 1½ inches from the left of the line; dot B is 2 inches; dot C is 4¼ inches along the line; dot D is 6½ inches; dot E is 7 inches from the left; and dot F is located 9 inches along the line.

Measure up 1¼ inches from dot A and mark that spot. Connect this spot with the left end of line 1 in a curve as shown in Illus. 88. This is line 2.

Illus. 88

Locate and mark the point 3 inches above dot B on line 1. Connect this point with another curve from the end of line 2.

Skip over dot C and move to dot D. Measure up from the line 3 inches and mark that location.

Now, go back to dot C. Set your compass so its points are 4 inches apart. Put the sharp point right on dot C; then use the pencil end of the compass to connect the end of line 3 with the mark above dot D. This curved line is line 4. If you don't have a compass, use the edge of an 8-inch pan lid to make line 4 or draw it freehand. Cruiser will fly either way. Measure up from dot E 1 inch and mark the point; then join that point with the end of line 4. This line, line 5, should be a curve and should pretty much match line 3.

Measure up 1 inch from dot F and mark that point. Connect it with the end of line 5 so line 6 is straight. Now measure up from the end of line 1, make a mark 2 inches above the line, and connect this mark with the end of line 1. This straight line is line 8. Yes, you drew line 8 before line 7. That's all right.

To construct line 7 set your compass points 2 inches apart (or use the bottom of a one-pound coffee can or something that size). Join the ends of lines 6 and 8 and you have line 7 in place.

While you have the compass points set 2 inches apart (or the coffee can handy), draw the half circle in Illus. 89 on a spare piece of material.

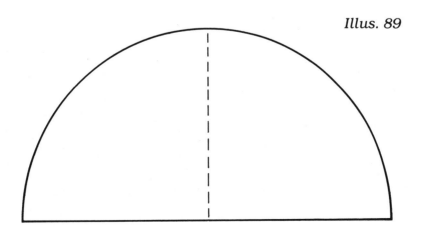

Illus. 89

Cruiser is ready to be cut out. Fold the material double along line 1. Remember to keep a firm hold so it won't slip when you cut out the outline, since both sides of the airplane need to be exactly the same.

When this is done cut out the half circle from Illus. 00. Fold it double so that it forms a quarter of a circle and is two sheets thick. Spread a little glue inside and press the two sides together. This is going to be the Cruiser's vertical stabilizer.

Fold down both wings along the dotted line in Illus. 88. Do the same for the horizontal stabilizer.

Slip the vertical stabilizer into the folded fuselage between the two halves of the horizontal stabilizer. Be sure the curved side is pointing towards the front of the airplane. When you glue the fuselage together, remember to put glue on both sides of the vertical stabilizer.

Once the glue is dry your Cruiser is ready to fly. This airplane should be easy to trim so that it flies in a pretty steady glide path. Its broad, rounded wings make it stable and steady.

With all the cut and glue airplanes be sure your horizontal stabilizers are at the same angle. This is one of the first things to check if your airplane seems to fly poorly. Having the stabilizers set differently will affect your airplane's performance.

You may want to decorate some of your paper airplanes. Magic markers are easy to use and look good when you are finished. Crayons are fine but may be a little harder to work with. With airplanes like the Cruiser it's easier to put on decorations before gluing them together.

PILOT'S CORNER

What Makes It Fly? There are four major things which influence the way an airplane flies, from commercial airliners to paper airplanes: thrust, drag, gravity and lift. The arrows in Illus. 90 indicate which way each one moves the airplane.

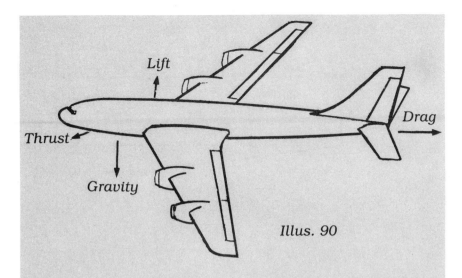

Illus. 90

Thrust   Thrust is the power which moves the airplane forward. Jet engines provide the thrust for a commercial airliner. Your hand gives your paper airplane its thrust.

Drag   Drag is the air pushing against the airplane as it flies forward. Since the wings have the greatest surface, they also tend to give the airplane the most drag. This is especially true when the nose of the plane tips up a bit; then the drag becomes extremely strong.

Gravity   Gravity is constantly pulling down on the airplane. This is true whether the plane is on the ground or flying. As you know, it's gravity which keeps things on the ground and which causes a thrown object such as a ball to come back to earth.

Lift   Lift is what combines with thrust to help get an airplane into the air. Once in the air, lift and thrust keep it flying. The airplane's wings provide the lift. It's an easy mistake to think that the air pushing up on the underside of the wings gives it lift, but it's the air that moves over the wings that creates lift.

   The faster the air moves, the less pressure it exerts on the top of the wing. It's this lower air pressure on top of the wings which really provides the plane with its lift.

   One way to get more lift is to curve the wings. By giving them a gentle curve so that the top of the wing seems slightly rounded, we improve lift. This makes the airplane fly better.

Stubborn

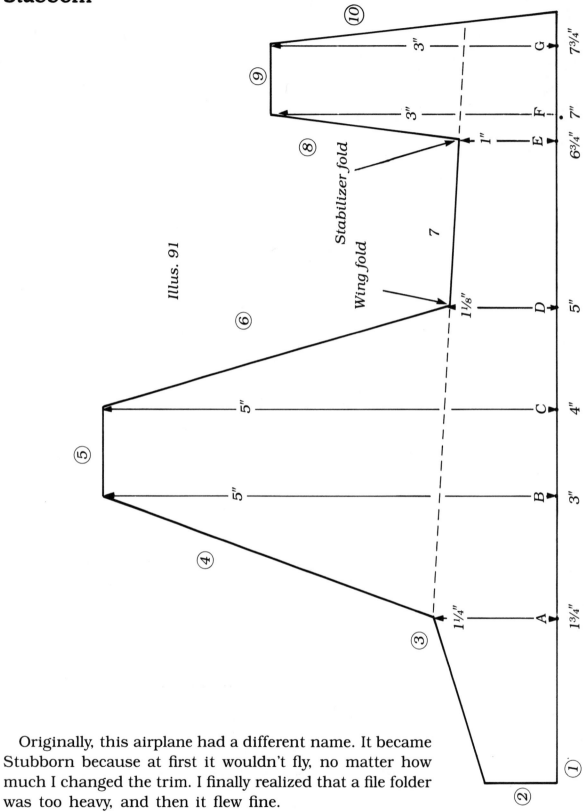

Illus. 91

Stabilizer fold

Wing fold

Originally, this airplane had a different name. It became Stubborn because at first it wouldn't fly, no matter how much I changed the trim. I finally realized that a file folder was too heavy, and then it flew fine.

Draw line 1 8 inches long on a sheet of stiff paper. (The brown paper bag paper is good for this.) Make certain this line is at least 5 inches from the edge of the paper.

Now place the dots along line 1 as shown in Illus. 91. Measuring from the left end of the line dot A is 1¾ inches over; dot B is 3 inches; dot C is 4 inches; and dot D is 5 inches from the left end of the line. Place dot E 6¾ inches from the left; dot F 7 inches from the left; and dot G 7¾ inches along line 1.

Draw line 2 straight up from the end of line 1 ¾ inch. Measure up from dot A on line 1 a distance of 1¼ inches, and mark that location. Now connect it with the end of line 2. This is line 3.

Next, measure up and mark a point 5 inches above dot B. Connect this point with the end of line 3 to construct line 4. From dot C measure up again 5 inches and mark this point. When it is joined to the end of line 4 you have line 5 in place.

Mark a point 1⅛ inches above dot D and join it with the end of line 5 to form line 6. Measure 1 inch above dot E and connect it with the end of line 6. Naturally this is line 7. Mark 3 inches above dot F so line 8 joins it and the end of line 7. Now make another mark 3 inches above dot G. Join this point with the end of line 8 to make line 9. Connect the end of line 9 with end of line 1 so you have the final line, line 10. Fold the material along line one so you are cutting out a double thickness.

After you have cut out Stubborn fold down the wings and horizontal stabilizer along the dotted lines in Illus. 91.

Stubborn's vertical stabilizer is shown in Illus. 92. Cut it out and place glue on both sides of the vertical stabilizer. Slip it into Stubborn's tail section so that the slanted line faces the front of the fuselage. (You can staple it into place if you are using staples.) Glue or staple the fuselage together and the Stubborn is ready to test.

Remember, if you design a paper airplane which won't perform, you should work at adjusting its trim until it flies or try different material and perhaps change the design. It is this sort of research which makes paper airplanes so much fun.

Illus. 92

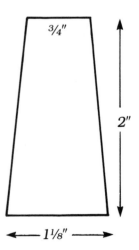

3/4"

2"

← 1⅛" →

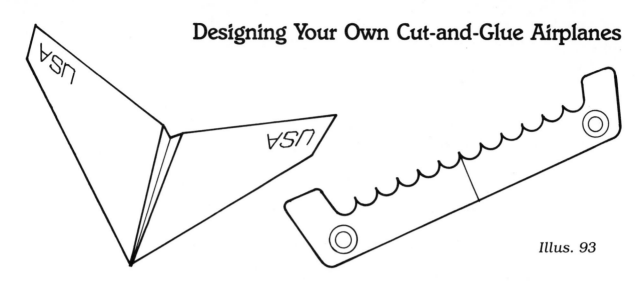

Designing Your Own Cut-and-Glue Airplanes

Illus. 93

You can design and test some airplanes of your own. There is absolutely no limit to the number of designs for paper airplanes of this type. The fuselage can be thick or thin; the nose curved, blunt, or slanted. The choice is yours.

Shape the wings and stabilizers any way you wish. We made airplanes with pointed, rounded, and straight wing tips but, there are countless other wing designs that will work.

If you enjoy this sort of research, let your imagination loose and have fun. Illus. 93 gives some possible wing shapes, but you will probably design ones which are more interesting.

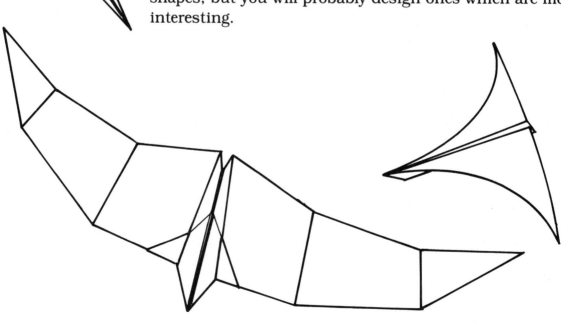

4.
New Designs

In 1987 newspaper articles told a strange, but true, tale. Officials from the Pentagon in Washington, D.C. were meeting with grade school children. (The Pentagon is that huge building where America's military planning takes place.)

High-ranking government officials and generals from the Pentagon needed an airplane for the future, and as part of their planning they asked grade school children for ideas. They not only talked to the students about what the airplane should be able to do, they asked them for design ideas.

At first this seemed completely impossible to believe; then the military planners explained that regular Air Force designers had so many ideas which they felt were right, it was difficult or even impossible to consider new ideas. These designers considered ideas that were already tried worthless. Some ideas were so different from anything now in production that the designers wouldn't consider them.

This is where the school children came in. They had no old ideas, and didn't know what was tried and failed.

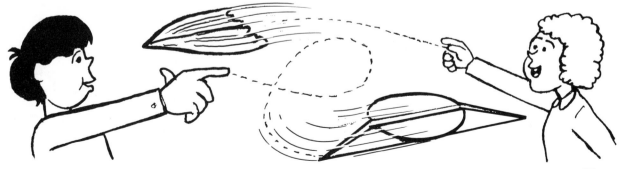

Their new ideas were so completely different that the designers had never thought of them. The students were not asked to tell how to make their new ideas work. All they were asked to provide was new and different ideas that might not have been considered before.

Did this plan work? It is too early to tell because the airplane won't be built until about the year 2000. When it is finished it will be part airplane and part spaceship. So, watch for it in the future, and remember that elementary students were asked for their ideas.

New Glide

No one will mistake New Glide for an airplane of the future. However, it's a good example of a new design. New Glide has no fuselage, just a pair of wings. The way you launch it is also a little different.

Begin construction of New Glide by folding a corner of a sheet of notebook paper over as though you were going to square the paper. (Take a quick look back to page 12 if you forgot how to square the paper.) But this time, don't cut off the extra paper. Instead, unfold the corner as in Illus. 94.

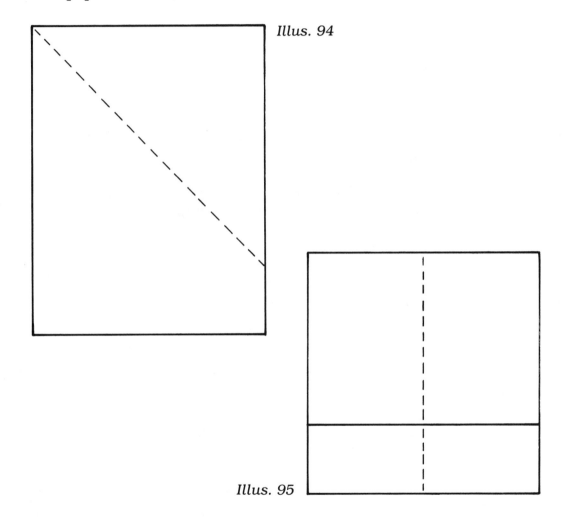

Illus. 94

Illus. 95

Fold over the part of the paper you normally cut off when making a square piece of paper; then fold the paper in the center. Crease this fold and unfold it so that it looks like Illus. 95.

Now fold the right-hand corner over, as in Illus. 96. Pay special attention to this fold. It extends exactly from the center almost to what will be the trailing edge of the wing.

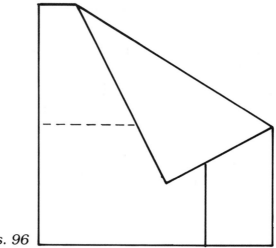

Illus. 96

Next, fold the opposite corner over and crease it into place. Be sure to line up the edge exactly with the fold you made in the last step, so the fold comes right to the nose point. Use a piece of tape to hold down this last fold. Place it as shown in Illus. 97. (You might also want to check your folds now.)

In the same illustration you see where to make a cut about ½ inch long. It's right along the center fold.

After making the cut, fold the two parts of the trailing edge over as shown in Illus. 98. Crease these down firmly, since they're not control surfaces.

Cut

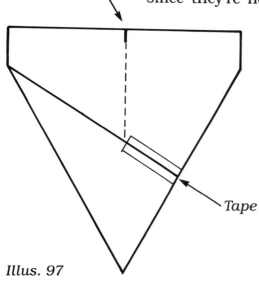

Tape

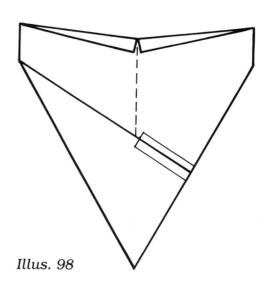

Illus. 97

Illus. 98

New Glide is now ready for launching. Lift its wings to give them a fairly good dihedral angle. Since New Glide has no fuselage you will launch it a bit differently.

Slip your index finger over the trailing edge so that your finger fits into the center fold, right over the cut you made. Illus. 99 shows how.

Illus. 99

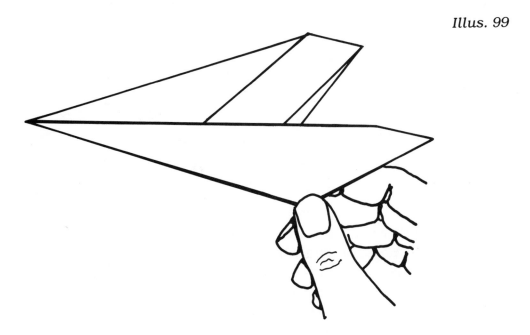

Launch New Glide with a gentle forward push. Don't snap your wrist. Just push the airplane into the air.

After you have flown New Glide a few times, you may want to experiment with the two rear flaps. Try making them into flaps or elevators by lifting them up a bit, or turning them down. When you are through experimenting you should see why your first flight with New Glide was with those two trailing edges creased down.

Needle Nose

Folding Needle Nose should be all the clue you need to discover the reason for its name.

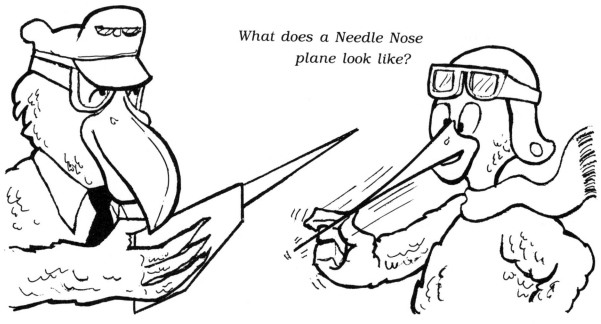

What does a Needle Nose plane look like?

Begin with a square sheet of notebook paper. Fold it in half, crease the fold; then unfold the paper. Fold one side into the center fold, exactly ¼ of the way from the paper's edge, and unfold it. Your paper should look like Illus. 100, with a crease in the paper's center and another halfway between the center and the edge of the paper.

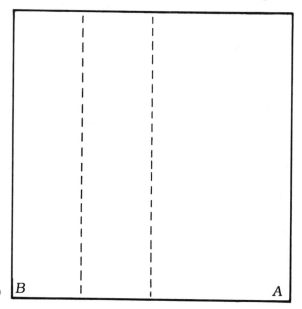

Illus. 100

B   A

Now fold corner A of the paper as shown in Illus. 101, but take a good look at the drawing before you make this fold. It begins right at the center fold, and does not quite extend to the other side of the paper. Corner A reaches exactly to the crease that's one-fourth of the way from the edge of the paper. Illus. 101 also shows your next fold.

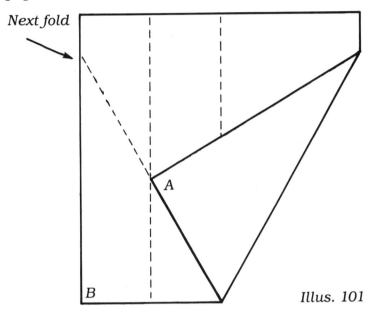

Illus. 101

Fold corner B along the dotted line so that Needle Nose will appear as seen in Illus. 102.

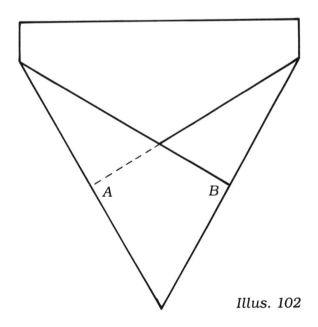

Illus. 102

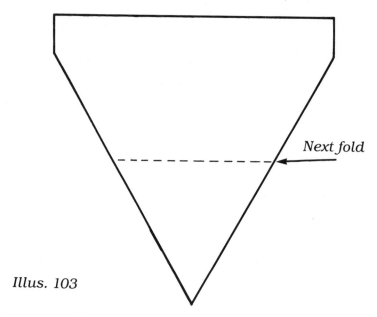

Next fold

Illus. 103

Now turn the paper over. Make the fold shown by the dotted line in Illus. 103; then look for the next fold shown

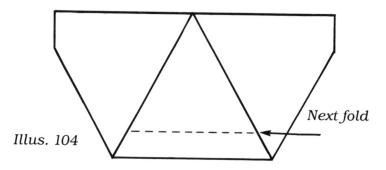

Next fold

Illus. 104

in Illus. 104. Fold the airplane's nose forward along the dotted line, so this plane looks like Illus. 105.

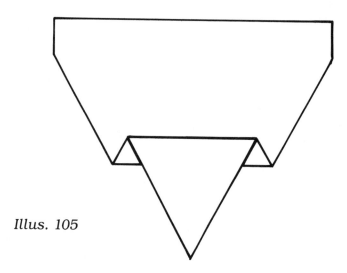

Illus. 105

Fold Needle Nose along the center fold (the one we made when we began this paper airplane). Folded up, your plane should look like Illus. 106. This illustration also shows the location for the wing folds. Before folding them, take a careful look at the dotted line. You'll see that the fold begins right at the point of the airplane's nose.

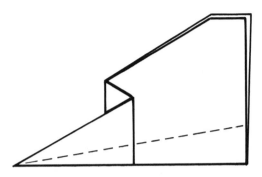

Illus. 106

When making the wing fold nearest you, fold the wing down along the dotted line. If you can't make the fold come exactly into the center of the nose don't worry about it. Get as close to the nose's center as you can. Since there are several layers of paper built up on the nose it may be difficult to make this fold exactly in the center of the nose.

When the wing closest to you is folded down into place, turn the airplane over and fold the second wing down into place. What you have now should look like Illus. 107.

Fold the wing nearest you up along the dotted line and crease it into place; then turn Needle Nose over and fold the second wing into place.

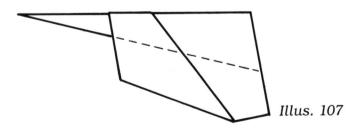

Illus. 107

Spread Needle's Nose's wings and it is ready for its first test flight. With all that folded paper towards the nose you will probably discover that this paper airplane flies just fine without any worry over trimming.

Here is a hint when flying paper airplanes such as this one. The long, pointed nose is likely to get smashed in a bit with hard landings, against walls, door frames, chairs, or any other hard object.

All you need to do to prepare your airplane for its next flight is to straighten out the nose and it is almost as good as new. However, you may want to give long, slender airplane noses a bit of extra strength.

To make these noses stronger, wrap a strip of tape around and around the pointed end of the airplane's nose. Be careful not to use too much tape since that may upset the airplane's trim. However, several inches of tape wrapped into place will help preserve a delicate nose from getting smashed in more often than is absolutely necessary.

Keep this hint in mind for the future, by the way.

PILOT'S CORNER

Trimming Tips   You know by now that placing paper clips at the nose will give a stalling airplane more weight forward, so that it has proper balance.

Sometimes it's better to move the paper clip back an inch or more from the nose. This is one of those things you discover only through trial and error during test flights, so don't be afraid to experiment. If you move a paper clip too far and the airplane crashes, no harm done. Just change the clip's location and take another test flight.

When you fly your paper airplanes outdoors you'll find that you usually must launch airplanes faster because the air movements are stronger.

Sky Cruiser

When this airplane is correctly trimmed, it certainly lives up to its name.

You'll need a pair of scissors and a sheet of notebook paper to build this plane. Begin Sky Cruiser by making a fold about one-third of the way from the end of the paper. Try to come as close as you can, but don't worry if you are off a fraction of an inch or so. Sky Cruiser will still fly just fine. Illus. 108 shows this fold, and the dotted line shows you your next fold. Fold the paper down the center along the dotted line. Illus. 109 shows your airplane at this point.

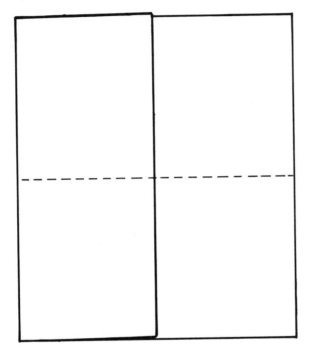

Illus. 108

Illus. 109

Take a look at Illus. 110 and note that corner A extends down about half an inch below the lower edge of the airplane's fuselage. This is one of the few times you make a fold which deliberately does not match the edge of a paper. Make this fold; then turn Sky Cruiser over and fold corner B down so that it matches corner A. Illus. 111 shows how the airplane looks at this stage.

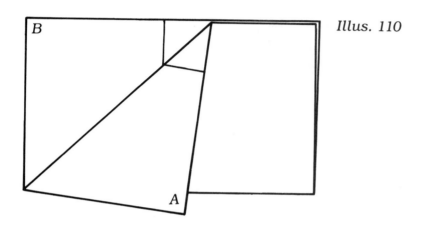

Illus. 110

Illus. 111

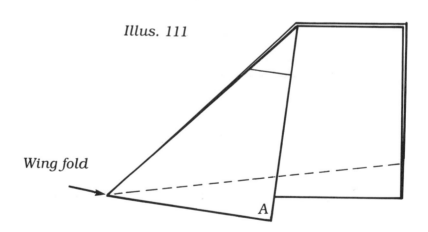

Wing fold

The dotted line in Illus. 111 shows the wing fold. Fold the wing closer to you down and crease it; then turn Sky Cruiser over and fold the second wing down into place. At this point your airplane looks like Illus. 112.

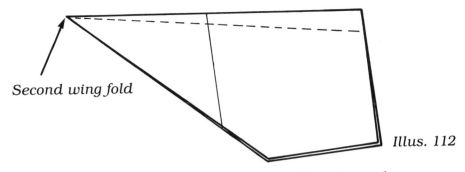

Second wing fold

Illus. 112

The dotted line in Illus. 112 shows where to make your next wing fold. Fold the wing nearer to you up along this dotted line; then turn the airplane over and fold the other wing up to match the first one, so that the plane matches Illus. 113.

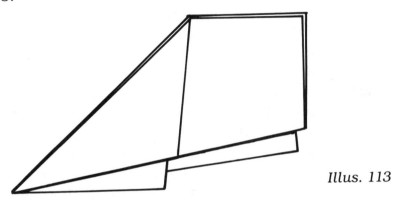

Illus. 113

Flatten the wings back into their original position, as in Illus. 114.

Now it's scissors time. Cut out the triangular piece of material (the blacked out area in Illus. 114). The point in the triangle should come exactly to the lower wing fold. Do this cutting carefully and make certain you cut just to the lower fold. Now cut the trailing edge flap shown with the

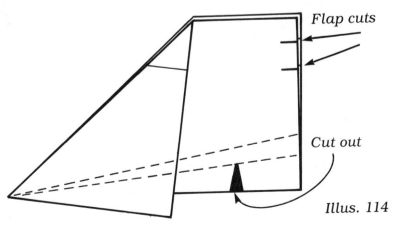

Flap cuts

Cut out

Illus. 114

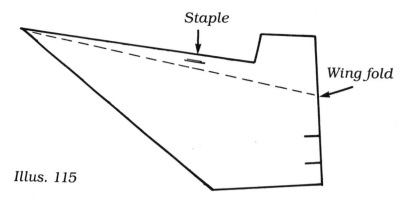

Staple

Wing fold

Illus. 115

arrows. These cuts are only about ¼ inch deep and 1 inch apart. (Remember, you don't have to be quite that exact unless you want to.)

Turn the rear portion of the fuselage inside out. Push up along the center fold so that the part of the fuselage to the rear of the triangular cut is now tucked up inside the fuselage. Now fold Sky Cruiser's wings back down along the lower wing fold. Your plane should look like Illus. 115. Staple the airplane as shown in Illus. 116. (The dotted line shows the second wing fold you made a little while ago.)

Lift the wings up along the previous fold (the dotted line in Illus. 115). Illus. 116 shows your finished airplane.

Bend the trailing edge flaps up so they stand nearly straight up and give your paper airplane its first test flight. Other than to adjust the flaps a bit you should not have to trim this great little airplane at all. It should take off and fly with a nearly straight glide path.

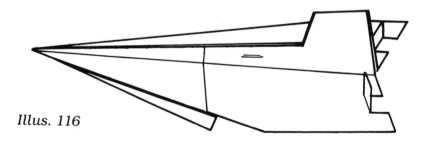

Illus. 116

Flying Bengal

This plane got its name from the Brentwood Bengals of Brentwood Middle School in Greeley, Colorado. An unknown Brentwood Bengal is responsible for bringing the Flying Bengal into this world.

Begin your Flying Bengal with a square piece of paper. Fold it diagonally along the center and crease the fold into place, as shown in Illus. 117. Fold down the wing near you on the dotted line you see in Illus. 117.

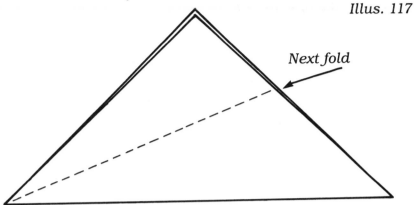

Illus. 117

Next fold

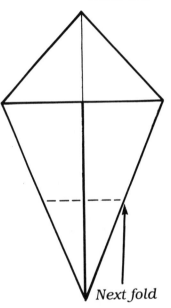

Illus. 118

Next fold

Turn the Flying Bengal over and fold the second wing down into place. Now, open the paper along the center fold, but leave the two wing folds in place. What we have now is shown in Illus. 118.

Fold the point of the nose back along the dotted line in Illus. 118. Note that the nose point comes exactly to the edges of the two wings we already folded. The dotted line in Illus. 119 tells you where to make the next fold. (Make sure you look carefully at the location of this line before you fold.) Fold the nose back along the dotted line. At this point you'll need a strip of tape about 3 or 4 inches long. Look at Illus. 120 to see where to place it.

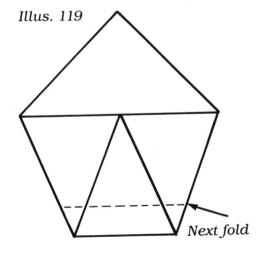

Illus. 119

Next fold

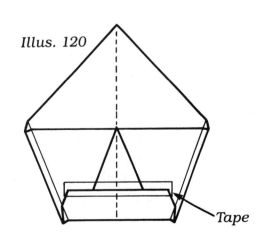

Illus. 120

Tape

83

Now fold the airplane along its center fold so that it appears as shown in Illus. 121.

The dotted line in Illus. 121 shows where to make the next fold. These folds are along the wings' leading edges and are called wing slats.

Illus. 121

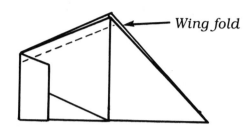

Wing fold

Turn the airplane over and make the second wing fold. Flatten out the center fold so that there is very little wing dihedral, and so that your plane looks like Illus. 122.

Illus. 122

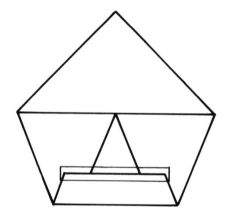

Launch the Flying Bengal by pinching in on the center fold to hold the airplane between your thumb and forefinger. Your first test flight will probably indicate the need for a paper clip on the airplane's nose for proper trim. Another way to launch this little fellow is to hold its tail with your forefinger on top of the center fold. Gently push the Flying Bengal into the air.

After some test flights, you may want to try giving the wings a little more dihedral angle and see how this affects its flight.

Try this research project. Up until now the wing slats have been folded up, so fold them down. Launch the airplane as before. The change should result in a long, gentle glide path.

Finally, launch your Flying Bengal backwards. Place your index finger on top of the nose fold with your thumb and middle finger under the nose. Launch the airplane a bit harder than when you pushed it into the air before.

You may find you need to launch the Flying Bengal at a little upwards angle when you do it this way. With this reverse launch you should expect this little airplane to make a loop for you and then go into a curving glide.

Flying Bengal?

Anything like the Flying Tigers?

Glide and Twist

With a name like Glide and Twist, the flight path of this paper airplane should not come as any great surprise. If you still have the tape and scissors handy from your last paper airplane, don't put them away. You will need a little piece of tape in order to finish the Glide and Twist.

The Glide and Twist is another paper airplane which uses a sheet of notebook paper. Fold the bottom 2 inches of the paper as shown in Illus. 123; then make a center crease as seen in Illus. 124. Unfold the paper after making the center crease.

Illus. 123

Illus. 124

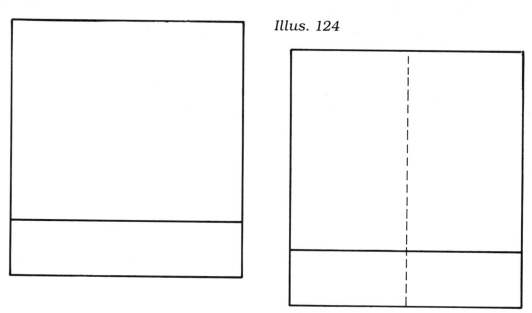

Fold corner A as shown in Illus. 125. Note that the fold begins right at the center crease and extends almost to the airplane's trailing edge. Fold corner B into place as in Illus. 126. This leaves corner B sticking out. Don't think something has gone wrong; it's supposed to be there.

Illus. 125

Illus. 126

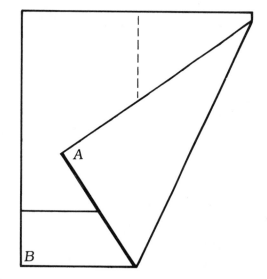

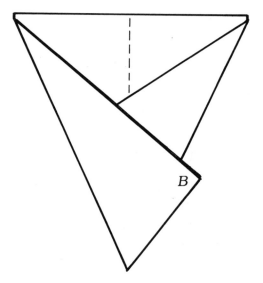

Turn your paper airplane over and crease into place corner B, as in Illus. 127. Tape this corner down firmly.

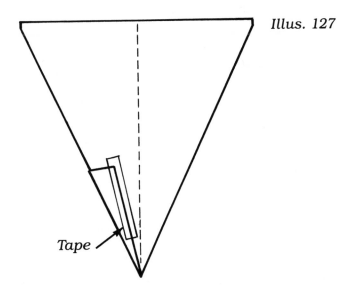

Illus. 127

Tape

Once corner B is taped into place refold the airplane along its center fold. Look at Illus. 128. With the scissors, make the cut indicated about 2 inches from the airplane's trailing edge, or tail. Make sure you can make this cut without cutting into the double thicknesses from corners A and B (the dotted line in Illus. 128). Make the cut about an inch deep.

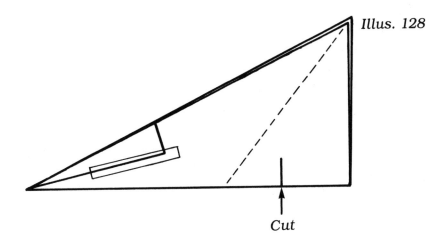

Illus. 128

Cut

After you make the cut, turn the paper that's behind the cut inside out by pushing up on the center fold. The paper will reverse itself. The dotted lines in Illus. 129 show where the folded paper will go.

Illus. 129

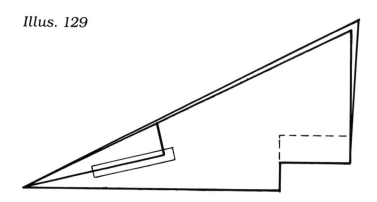

Your Glide and Twist is now ready for launching. If you get more Twist than Glide try trimming with a paper clip.

After a few flights you might want to put some control flaps along the trailing edge. If you put flaps in, don't make the cuts too deep; about ¼ inch should be right.

5.
Multi-Part Airplanes

We've already made some multi-part airplanes in Chapter 3. Any paper airplane which uses two or more pieces of paper is a multi-part airplane, and the planes in this chapter all use at least two pieces of paper. Multi-part paper airplanes are fun to make and fly because they are entirely different from most airplanes.

Illus. 130

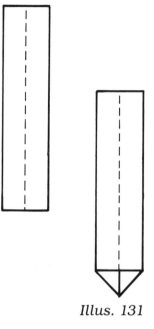

Dipper

The Dipper has a really special sort of flight. When all goes well, the Dipper begins its flight with a nice, calm glide; then gives a little dip while in mid-flight and finally comes in for a smooth landing.

Let's get the easy part out of the way first. Cut a piece of paper about 8½ inches long and 2¼ inches wide. Make a center fold in the paper the long way; then unfold this strip so that it looks like Illus. 130.

Now fold the two corners in to the center crease as Illus. 131 shows. Leave the corners folded in place and set this strip of paper aside for a minute or two.

Make the main part of the Dipper from a sheet of notebook paper. Begin by folding one corner into place; then fold the other corner over and crease it, as in Illus. 132.

Illus. 131

Unfold the paper so that it lies flat and turn it over. Fold the bottom up so that it meets the corners you just folded. Check Illus. 133 for help.

Illus. 132

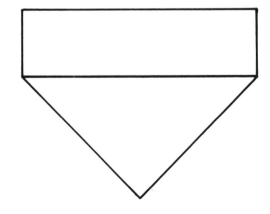

Illus. 133

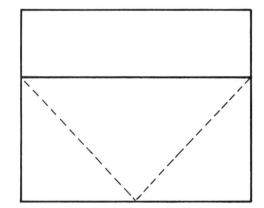

Unfold the paper and turn it over. It should look very much like Illus. 134. The arrows show where to push in. As you push in, work the bottom of the paper upwards so that the Dipper comes together to look like Illus. 135. Since you have done this sort of folding in several previous paper airplanes you should be pretty good at it by now.

Illus. 134   Illus. 135

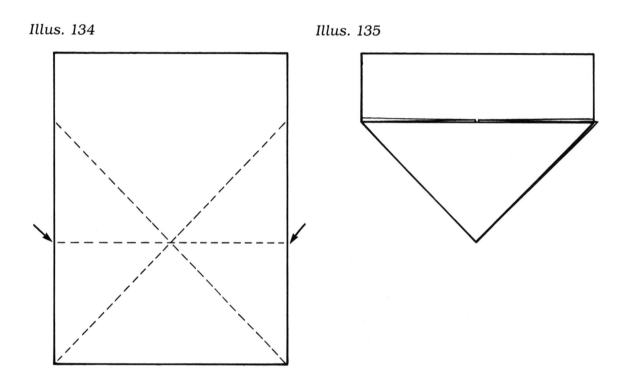

Fold the Dipper as in Illus. 136 and crease it well; then unfold this last center line fold.

Illus. 136

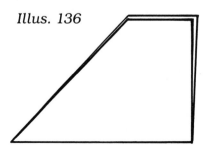

Now you need the narrow strip of paper you folded a few minutes ago.

Oh, thanks.

Carefully slip this narrow strip down the Dipper's center line. Make sure the two center line folds match exactly.

Push the pointed end of the narrow strip of paper all the way into the point of the Dipper's nose, so that it looks like Illus. 137. The dotted line across the airplane's nose shows where to make the next fold, about an inch behind the point of the nose. Fold the nose point back along the dotted line and crease it very well.

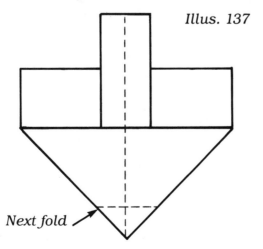

Illus. 137

Next fold

Illus. 138

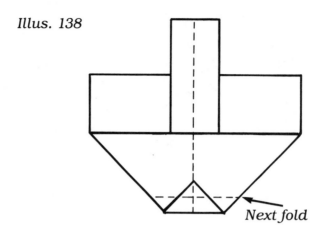

Next fold

Your next fold is the dotted line in Illus. 138. Make the second nose fold and be sure to crease it into place. After all, you don't want the Dipper's nose to come unfolded while in flight. Illus. 139 shows where we are at this point.

Illus. 139

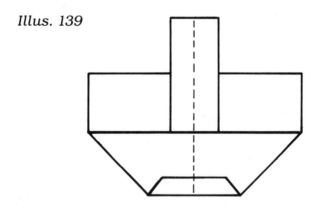

Refold the airplane along its center fold. Be careful or the nose will twist and not fold exactly. There are now so many folds of paper built up in the nose section that it is quite thick and may be a little stubborn when you fold it. Your paper airplane now appears in Illus. 140.

Illus. 140

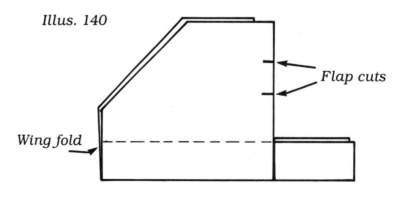

Flap cuts

Wing fold

The dotted line indicates where to make your wing fold. Note that it is exactly along the edge of the narrow strip of paper. Now, make the cuts on the trailing edges of the wings for control flaps. These cuts should be about ⅜ inch each. Make the flap cuts, but don't fold the flaps. By making the flap cuts now, you can cut both wings at the same time, so the flaps will be exactly the same for each wing. Although you don't have to be quite so exact it never hurts to be as nearly perfect as possible.

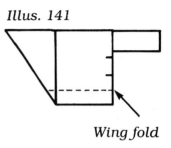

Illus. 141

Wing fold

Fold the rear wing down along the dotted line in Illus. 141; then turn the airplane over and fold down the other wing. The dotted lines in Illus. 141 show our final wing fold; so fold the wing next to you up along the dotted line. Turn the airplane over and fold the other wing up.

Spread the wings and turn both flaps up. Your Dipper looks very much like Illus. 142. With all those nose folds the Dipper is already pretty much in trim.

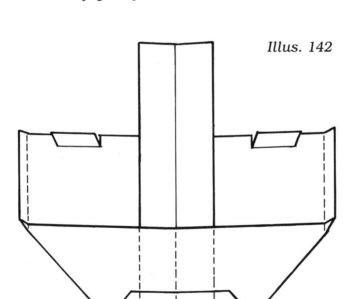

Illus. 142

Launch it a few times and see how it performs. After several test flights, see how your airplane behaves if you add one or even two paper clips to its nose.

Once you find exactly the proper trim your Dipper should reward you with a smooth glide, a dip in its flight path, and a smooth landing.

V.T.

This time we'll begin with the forward section.

A sheet of notebook paper will be the airplane's forward part. Fold one corner over as shown in Illus. 143.

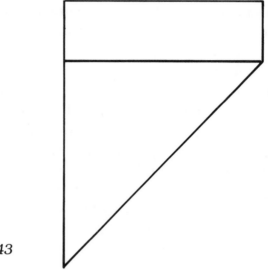

Illus. 143

Yes, you guessed it! Fold the other corner over so our airplane-to-be looks like Illus. 144.

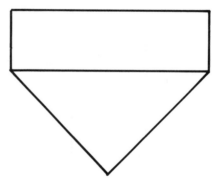

Illus. 144

Now unfold the paper and turn it over. Fold the bottom up so that it comes exactly at the point the two previous folds meet each other. You can see this in Illus. 145.

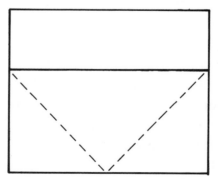

Illus. 145

Unfold this fold and turn the paper over again. This step is shown in Illus. 146. The arrows tell where to push in order to get the paper to fold in on itself. With this accomplished your V.T. should look like Illus. 147.

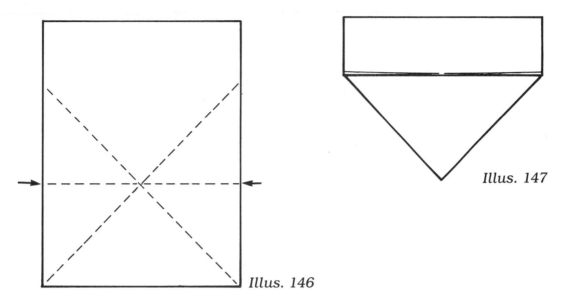

Illus. 146

Illus. 147

Fold your paper airplane in half and crease the center, as in Illus. 148. Set this part of your V.T. to one side.

Illus. 148

What does V.T. mean?

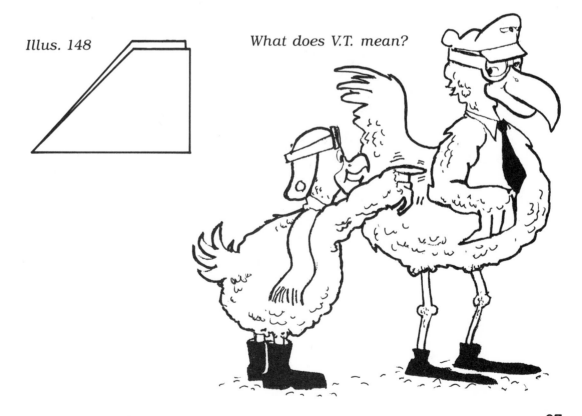

Fold a second sheet of notebook paper the long way to make a center crease, as in Illus. 149.

Do you still have the scissors handy? You'll need them for the next step. (If you have to get up to find them, better grab your roll of tape at the same time.)

Hold the two thicknesses of paper together tightly so the bottom one does not slip when you cut. Cut out the shaded area in Illus. 150, the long, narrow piece of material below the cut out section measures about 1¼ inches × 5 inches. As we have said before, these measurements do not have to be exact. A difference of a fraction of an inch will not ruin your V.T. It is only the really big mistakes which cause problems. Unfold this part of the V.T. and it will look like Illus. 151.

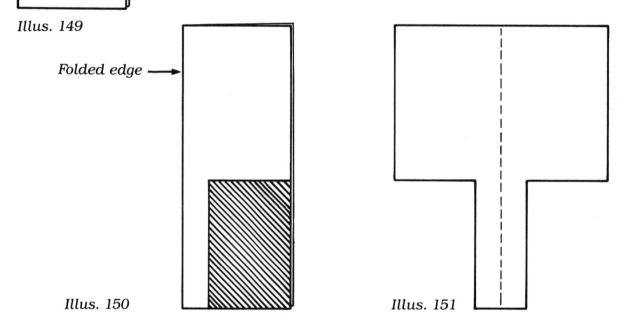

Illus. 149

Folded edge ⟶

Illus. 150

Illus. 151

Fold the right-hand nose corner in to the center crease; then do the same for the left-hand corner. When these two folds have been completed the nose point looks like Illus. 152.

Make the next fold as shown in Illus. 153. Be sure the point comes exactly to the center fold.

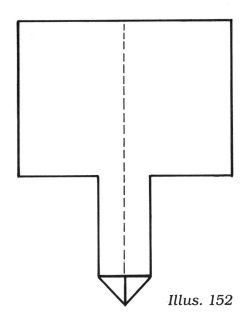

Illus. 152

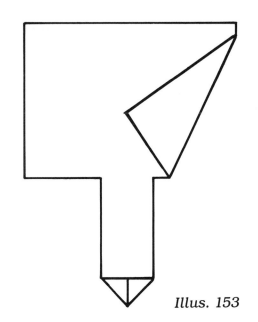

Illus. 153

Make a similar fold for the opposite side of the tail section. Use a small strip of tape to hold these two folds in place, as shown in Illus. 154.

Refold this part of your V.T. along its center line. It should look very much like Illus. 155. The two lines in the trailing edge tell you where to cut your control flaps. Hold the two sides of the V.T.'s trailing edge together when you make these cuts. That way you only have to make one pair of cuts and flaps in both sections are in exactly the same place which should help your paper airplane's trim.

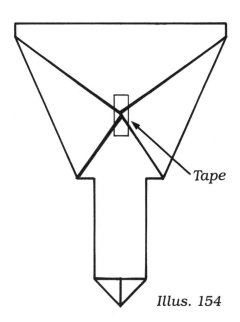

Tape

Illus. 154

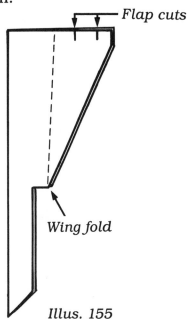

Flap cuts

Wing fold

Illus. 155

After making the flap cuts, fold the wing near you down along the dotted line; then turn the airplane over and fold the second wing down into place.

Open your V.T. out flat so that it appears as seen in Illus. 156.

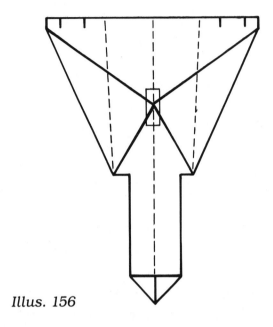

Illus. 156

Slip the nose point of this section of your paper airplane into the nose point of the part we first worked on. Be sure to push the tail section's nose point all the way into the leading section, as you see in Illus. 157.

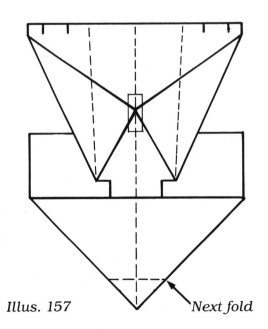

Illus. 157   *Next fold*

The dotted line across the nose in this drawing indicates your next fold. Fold V.T.'s nose back and crease it into place. Illus. 158 shows how V.T. looks at this stage, and also shows where to make your next fold. Make this second fold along the dotted line.

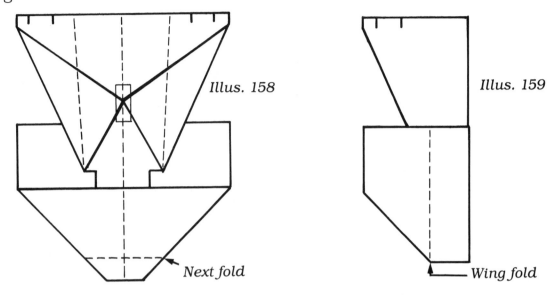

Illus. 158

Next fold

Illus. 159

Wing fold

Now refold the entire paper airplane along its center line. Your V.T. can be seen in Illus. 159. The dotted line indicates the position of your next wing fold. When you make this wing fold be sure you fold down only the wing on the front section of the airplane. The trailing section of the airplane already has its wing folds in place.

But what does V.T. mean?

Fold down the rear wing and crease the fold into place. Turn the airplane over and fold the second wing into place. By now your airplane should look like Illus. 160.

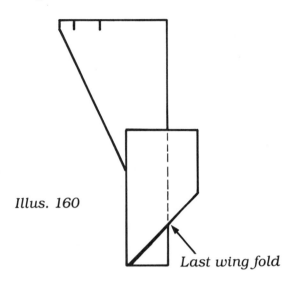

Illus. 160

Last wing fold

The dotted lines in Illus. 160 show where to make the last wing folds. Fold the wing that's nearer to you up along the dotted line. Turn the airplane over and fold the other wing up. Open the wings out into place, bend both trailing edge flaps up and your V.T. is ready to launch.

After a flight or two, experiment with the airplane's trim by adjusting the dihedral angle for both sets of wings. The angle of the upright edges of the front set of wings also influences V.T.'s flight characteristics.

If you launch V.T. outside, try launching it directly into the wind. When you do this, you will probably discover that your airplane tends to start almost straight up for the first several feet of its flight. That is how it got the name V.T. It stands for vertical take off.

Oh, that's what it means.

102

The interesting thing about this airplane is that it goes for a vertical take off only when launched directly into a fairly stiff breeze. At other times it seems to forget all about starting its flight upwards. Fly it a few times both inside and outside and see how your V.T. performs under different conditions.

PILOT'S CORNER

Roll Here's a good aeronautical term (actually any word that refers to flying or airplanes is called aeronautical.) A roll is when an airplane tips to one side or the other during flight, as in Illus. 161. You can correct a roll by making sure both wings have exactly the same dihedral angle. An airplane whose wings have no dihedral may also roll. In that case, give them a bit of an angle.

You may not want to correct a roll. Sometimes an airplane which rolls to one side and goes into an gentle turn will do exactly what you want it to do.

Roll

Illus. 161

Pitch Pitch is another good aeronautical word. Look at Illus. 162 and you'll see this means the airplane's nose is either going upwards or downwards. To correct this you need to change the craft's center of gravity. Adding a paper clip or moving the clip one way or the other is a quick way to do this.

Pitch

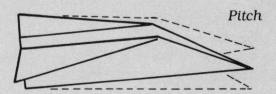

Illus. 162

Yaw When the airplane's nose turns either right or left (as in Illus.163) pilots say the plane is yawing. Yaw is a great word to remember and impress your friends with. To correct yawing make sure the vertical stabilizer is straight up and down. If your airplane does not have a vertical stabilizer you can sometimes add one by cutting it out and gluing it into place.

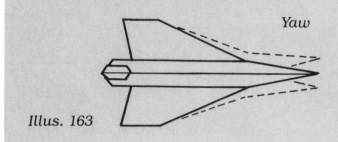

Yaw

Illus. 163

Super Glide

This next multi-part airplane requires two sheets of notebook paper. You'll also need four strips of tape.

Fold both sheets of paper in half the long way, crease the center lines and unfold them. Both sheets now look like Illus. 164.

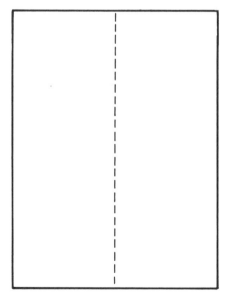

Illus. 164

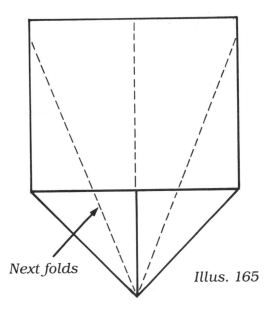

Next folds　　　*Illus. 165*

Take one sheet and fold two corners as shown in Illus. 165. Make certain each corner's edge comes right to the center line.

Now make the folds shown by the dotted lines in Illus. 165. When you fold along the dotted lines be certain the edge of each fold goes right to the center line. Illus. 166 shows your Super Glide at this point, and also shows where to put a strip of tape to hold the two sides firmly together.

Put this part of your newest paper airplane to one side. It's time to fold the second part of the Super Glide.

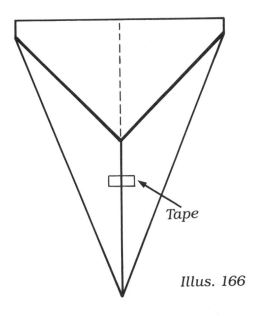

Tape

Illus. 166

Fold both lower corners in to the center line, as in Illus. 167. This is just like the first step you took with the other section of the airplane.

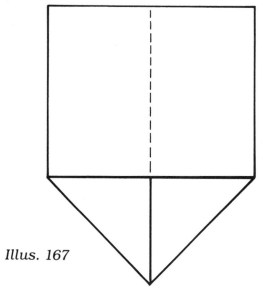

Illus. 167

Now fold both sides of this section of your Super Glide in to the center line. Illus. 168 shows your airplane after these folds were made. Just in case you have any problem with this step, check back to Illus. 165 where the two dotted lines give the location of these folds.

Next, refold the paper along the center fold. It should look just like Illus. 169 and the dotted line indicates the wing fold which you are ready to make. Fold the first wing down.

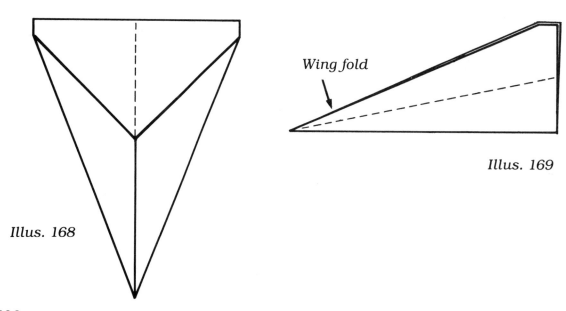

Wing fold

Illus. 169

Illus. 168

Turn the airplane over and fold down and crease the other wing. Lift up into flying position, so that the top view of the airplane looks like Illus. 170. You'll also see where to put a strip of tape to hold the wings together.

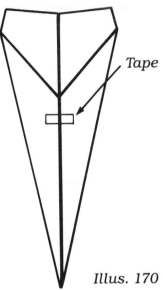

Illus. 170

Now place the first part of Super Glide flat and turn the other section over so that the side with the tape is facing downwards. Place this portion of your airplane on top of the first part. Be sure to put the center lines right on top of each other. Your Super Glide now looks like Illus. 171. It also shows you where to put the two strips of tape that will hold the two parts of your airplane together. These strips should be about 2 inches long.

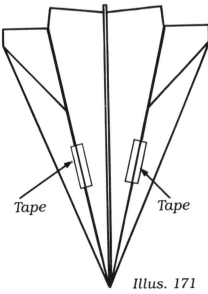

Illus. 171

Turn the Super Glide over. Grasp the fuselage firmly and launch your airplane.

Super Glide will give you some of the smoothest gliding flights you have had from your growing paper air force. After a flight or two you should see how it got its name.

Skinny

Keep your scissors and tape handy to construct Skinny.

Skinny is a three-piece airplane. One sheet of notebook paper and a smaller piece of stiff material are needed. A 3 × 5 file card is just perfect, but any stiff paper will do the job.

Let's begin with the file card. Fold it down the middle so that it looks like Illus. 172. Now cut away the shaded area in Illus. 173.

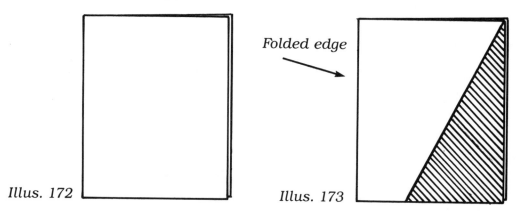

Folded edge

Illus. 172   Illus. 173

This piece of Skinny, which will become the airplane's nose section, now looks like Illus. 174 and the dotted line indicates the next fold. Fold down the side next to you; then turn the paper over and make a similar fold on the other side.

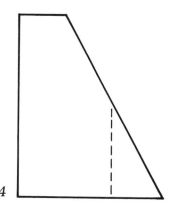

Illus. 174

You have just constructed a pair of vertical stabilizers. The difference between these stabilizers and most others is that these are located on the airplane's nose rather than as part of the tail assembly. Set this piece to one side.

Cut the sheet of notebook paper in half so that you have two pieces of material, each about 8½ × 5½ inches. The dotted line in Illus. 175 indicates this cut.

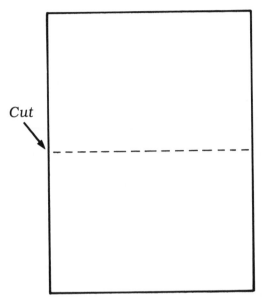

Cut

Illus. 175

Place one of the pieces you just cut in front of you so the width (the 8½-inch part) is towards you. Begin rolling this paper. Try to leave a hollow center which is about ¼ inch across. Roll the paper tightly until all the sheet has become part of the roll.

Use two or three pieces of tape along the loose edge to keep the paper from unrolling. Illus. 176 shows you where to place the strips of tape. This is Skinny's fuselage.

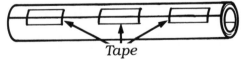

Tape

Illus. 176

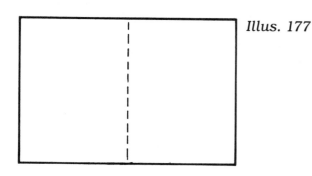

Illus. 177

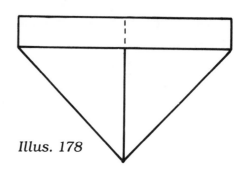

Illus. 178

Fold the second sheet of paper down the middle to locate the center line. It looks like Illus. 177 when you unfold it.

Next, fold in both the lower corners. Be sure the edge of each fold comes exactly to the center fold. Crease both folds well. What you have now can be seen in Illus. 178.

Fold the paper back along its center fold so that it appears as in Illus. 179. Fold down the wing near you along the dotted line; then turn this part of Skinny over and fold the second wing down into place. Illus. 180 should match your project at this point.

Illus. 179

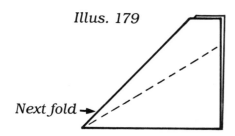

Next fold →

Illus. 180

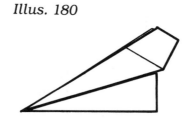

After you have creased these wing folds return them to the way they were before you folded them down, as in Illus. 181. Hold the wings together tightly and make the cut shown by the line in Illus. 181. Cut into the material about ½ inch.

After making the cuts, fold both flaps of material back down. Check with Illus. 180 to see if your airplane looks pretty much like the original.

Cut

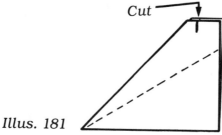

Illus. 181

Open this section of your airplane so that the center fold and the edges of the two wing folds touch the tabletop.

Now place the fuselage tube on top of the center fold, about 3 inches from the leading point of the folded paper. Illus. 182 shows Skinny at this point.

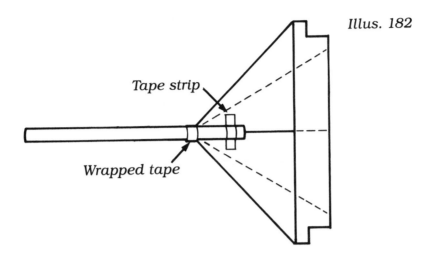

Illus. 182

Tape strip

Wrapped tape

Attach the tail section to the fuselage tube with a strip of tape as shown in Illus. 182. Don't let the wings pull away from the center fold while you do this. If they give you a problem, put a bit of tape onto them to hold them in place until you get the fuselage attached.

Put another strip of tape at the point of the tail section long enough to wrap around the fuselage tube and the tip of the tail section. You might want to put several pieces around the tail and tube while you are at it, so Skinny's tail won't start flapping while in flight.

It's now time to attach the nose piece. Take a good look at Illus. 183 before you begin taping things together. The nose section fits on top of the fuselage tube. Notice that with the center fold on top of the fuselage tube the nose section slopes down on either side. This downwards slope is just the opposite of the dihedral angle most paper airplanes use.

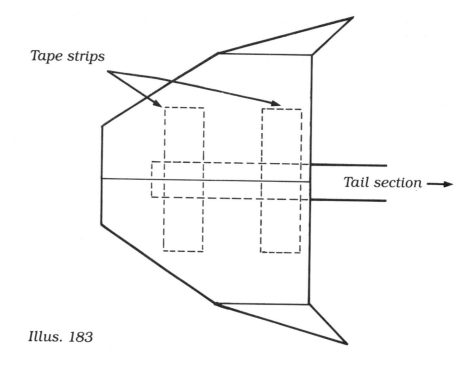

Tape strips

Tail section →

Illus. 183

Make sure the end of the fuselage tube extends about 2 inches over the nose piece. Use two pieces of tape to attach the nose to the fuselage. The dotted lines in Illus. 183 show where to place the tape (the lines are dotted because the tape is actually under the nose piece).

Skinny is now ready for launching. If it needs a paper clip for balance, the clip is easy to attach: just slip it over one side of the fuselage tube and it should never come off.

Once your newest paper airplane is trimmed and its stabilizers are adjusted to their best angle Skinny should reward you with an even glide path.

After the first few crashes into the walls and the furniture, Skinny's nose may begin to show signs of wear. Try folding several layers of tape over it to make it stronger. Even another thickness of stiff material over the front part of your airplane's nose section would work. If you do this it will change the airplane's balance a bit, but just retrim Skinny and you'll be able to send it off for another glide through the living room or across the lawn.

6.

Modification and Experimental Designs

A modification is a change in an airplane's design. Some paper airplanes in this chapter are modifications because they are somewhat like other airplanes but with some interesting differences. Others are experimental because they aren't like anything.

In many ways most paper airplanes are experimental in some way. Every time you change control surfaces you perform an experiment of sorts. But just wait until you fold and fly some of the paper airplanes in this chapter. Some of them are really different!

Gemini

As you most likely know already, Gemini refers to twins. The twins in the Gemini paper airplane are its twin tail sections. You'll need the tape and scissors as well as a sheet of notebook paper.

Make the fold seen in Illus. 184. This fold should be about ¾ inch from the paper's lower edge. After you crease the first fold into place, fold the paper over two more times as shown by the two dotted lines in Illus. 184.

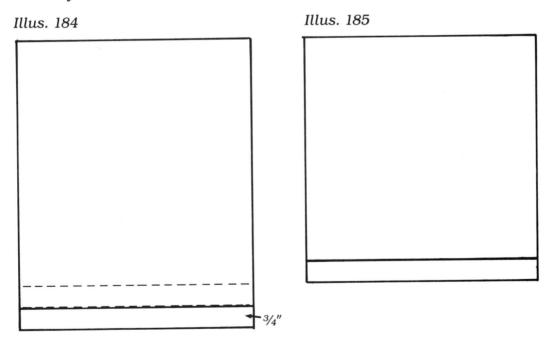

Illus. 184 *Illus. 185*

With these two folds completed your Gemini looks like Illus. 185. The dotted line shows your next step, the center fold.

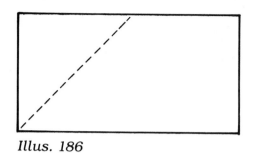

Illus. 186

After making the center fold, fold along the dotted line in Illus. 186. Fold the nose corner down and crease it into place; then turn the Gemini over and fold down the other nose corner as well. Your paper airplane should look like Illus. 187. The dotted line locates the next fold. Make the wing fold, crease it into place, and turn your airplane over and fold the other wing in the same manner. Once both wings have been folded down and creased we have reached Illus. 188.

Illus. 187

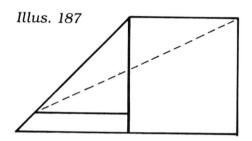

Before folding any more take just a second to tape the wing as shown in Illus. 188. Naturally, you need to turn the Gemini over and tape its other wing at the same time.

Now make the second wing fold. The dotted line in Illus. 188 shows it. Fold and crease the wing nearer to you, just as you always do. Then, turn the airplane over and fold the other wing. When the two wings are both folded, your Gemini should look like Illus. 189.

Tape

Illus. 188

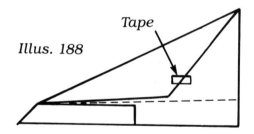

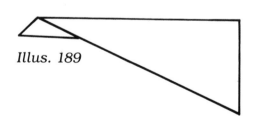

Illus. 189

Flatten out this last wing fold; then open Gemini along its center fold so that it appears like Illus. 190.

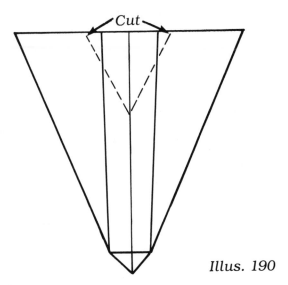

Illus. 190

In this drawing you see a cut along the center line. Cut in about 3 inches (¼ inch more or less than 3 inches won't bother Gemini). Once this cut is made, fold the tail section along the dotted lines.

By folding these two pieces of the airplane's tail section you are creating a pair of vertical stabilizers, one for each of Gemini's twin tails.

Illus. 191 shows the aircraft after the folds have been made. Use two short pieces of tape to fasten the vertical stabilizers into position as shown.

Fold both wing edges down along the dotted lines shown in Illus. 191.

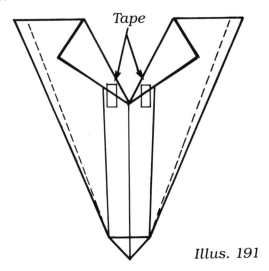

Illus. 191

Pull the fuselage together and lift the wings into place so Gemini looks like Illus. 192. Note how the vertical stabilizers now stand up ready to do their job.

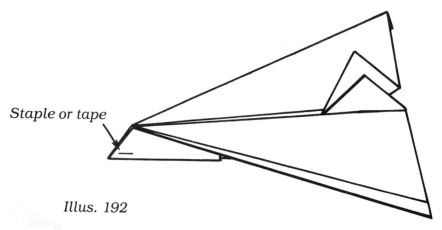

Staple or tape

Illus. 192

Put a staple or wrap a piece of tape in the airplane's nose as shown in Illus. 192. Adjust the wings so they have a little dihedral angle and launch Gemini for its first trial flight.

By bending the outer wing folds up or down a little you can make adjustments in the Gemini's flight path. After you have flown this paper airplane a few times, you may want to give it a pair of control flaps on the trailing edges of its wings. With Gemini, you won't have to have big flaps, so the smaller the better.

PILOT'S CORNER

Negative Dihedral When the dihedral angle of the nose section is down, rather than up, the plane has a negative dihedral. (There won't be a test on this at the end of the book, but you can use this word to impress your friends and parents.)

Lean Machine

This modified Dart comes to you from London, England.

Your first step is to cut a piece of notebook paper into two pieces. One of them should be 11 × 5½ inches in size. The other should be 2 × 3 inches. Begin with the larger piece.

Make a center fold and crease it into place; then unfold the paper so that it looks like Illus. 193. The dotted lines show your next folds.

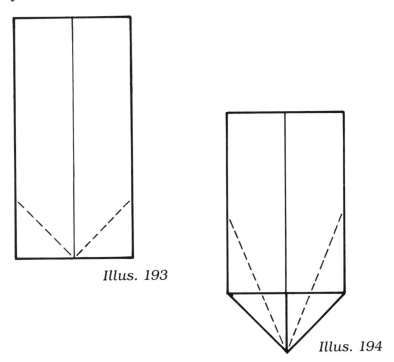

Illus. 193

Illus. 194

After you make the two folds shown by these dotted lines, your Lean Machine looks like Illus. 194. The next two folds should look familiar.

Now refold the Lean Machine along its center fold in Illus. 195. Fold the wing nearer you down along the dotted line; then turn the airplane over and fold the second wing down. At this point the Lean Machine looks like Illus. 196.

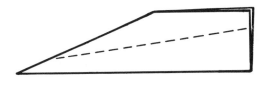

Illus. 195

Illus. 196

Now let's deal with the 2 × 3-inch piece of paper.

What you're actually making with this small piece of paper is the world's fanciest and most complicated paper clip. When you get it folded it's going to do the same job you have been doing with the paper clip you use on some airplanes.

Begin with the 2-inch side of the paper facing you. Fold the top down to the bottom so that it looks like Illus. 197. The two dotted lines in this illustration show your next folds, but don't make those folds until you read ahead:

Fold corner A towards you and crease the fold. Now fold corner B away from you. This puts corner B behind the rest of the paper after the fold is complete.

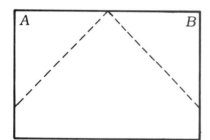

Illus. 197

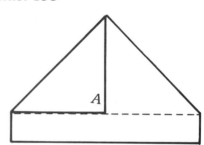

Illus. 198

Look at the dotted line in Illus. 198. You know you have two sections of paper here to fold. Fold the front section of the paper forward; then fold the back part of the paper over the rear of the nose cone. It should look like Illus. 199. (Looks kind of like a fancy party hat, doesn't it?)

Fold the dotted line in Illus. 199 towards you. Tuck the end into the opening behind the folded section so that your nose cone looks like Illus. 200.

Now fold the other corner back along the other dotted line, and tuck the end into the space behind the folded paper just as you did a minute ago. Your completed nose cone should look like Illus. 201.

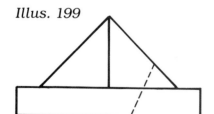

Illus. 199

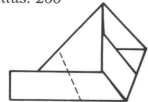

Illus. 200

Illus. 201

Slip the nose point of your Lean Machine into the opening at the base of the nose cone. Be sure the nose point goes all the way in.

Illus. 202 shows your plane ready for flight. Launch it with a quick snap of the wrist. It should fly far and fast.

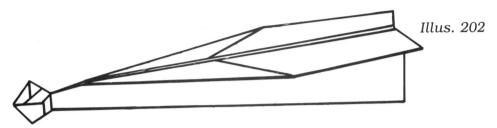

Illus. 202

PILOT'S CORNER

Trimming Tips   When the plane noses up and stalls either add nose weight or bend the elevators on the horizontal stabilizer down a bit. If you have a one-piece airplane in which the wing and stabilizer are together, try making control flaps on the trailing edge and bending them down slightly. When the plane noses down, remove some nose weight or bend the elevators up a little.

To keep an airplane from curving to the right too much, lower the right aileron or the trailing edge of the right wing. You could also bend the rudder to the left, or bend the left aileron up.

Everything you do to your paper airplane has some affect on the way it performs. You know by now that bending a control surface up will have the opposite effect of bending it down. So, if your airplane curves to the left you do just the opposite than when it curved to the right. To stop a left curve lower the left aileron, bend the rudder towards the right, or bend the right aileron up.

Floater

Shortly after the Second World War a completely new idea in aircraft was introduced. It was known as the Flying Wing. This huge airplane was built in the form of a giant wing. People marvelled that it could fly.

Your Floater is similar to the Flying Wing. Like that famous old plane, your paper airplane will make long flights, longer than you might expect, especially when it picks up just the right air currents.

Start with a sheet of notebook paper. Fold one of the long sides over ½ inch. Crease the fold into place, and just fold the paper over and over on itself. Crease each fold well so that it stays in place. The folded portion will become the leading edge of your wing.

Keep building up thicknesses of paper until the paper is 4 inches from the leading edge to the trailing edge of the wing. Illus. 203 shows the Floater at this stage of construction.

Make a 1 inch cut with your scissors on either side of the wing, 2 inches from the trailing edge. Illus. 203 shows where. After making the cuts, fold up the 2 vertical stabilizers. These folds are the dotted lines in Illus. 203.

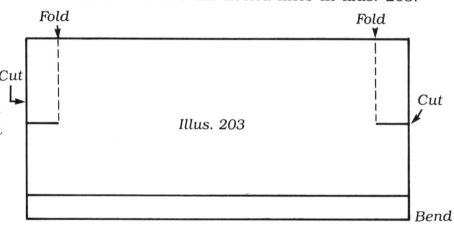

Illus. 203

Now, bend the leading edge of the wing in its center. Don't fold the wings together as we usually do; just crimp it or bend it a bit. This bend keeps the rolled paper from unrolling. A strip of tape can also do the job if needed. The bend or crimp in the wing's leading edge also gives the wing a bit of dihedral.

That's all there is to the Floater.

To launch this experimental paper airplane, all you need to do is hold it up and very gently push it into flight. Don't be tempted to launch it with a quick snap of your wrist— that's not the Floater's style.

Push it into the air and watch its easy gliding flight. Even slight air currents will lift the Floater a few inches or even a foot while in flight. This paper airplane won't set any speed records but when everything goes well it will glide a lot farther than most people expect.

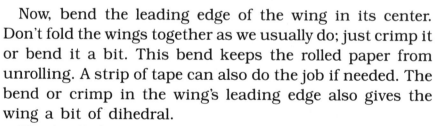

Hey! A floating flying wing!

122

Diver

The Diver is a playful little airplane. Sometimes it glides a little distance, hesitates, then dives almost straight to the ground. At other times it just glides in a semi-circle and lands gently. With a paper clip for nose trim it usually takes off on a long, almost straight, glide path.

Cut a sheet of notebook paper in half so that you have a piece of material 5½ inches × 8½ inches. (If you want to construct another, larger, Diver using a full sheet of paper it will fly just fine.)

Fold the paper to locate the center fold; then unfold the paper. Now fold both nose corners in towards the center fold as in Illus. 204.

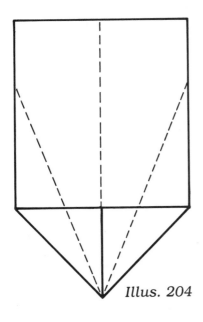

Illus. 204

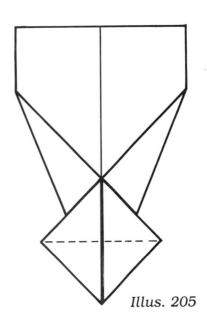

Illus. 205

Look carefully at the dotted lines in Illus. 204. Make these folds and crease them; then unfold them. Unfold the corners you made before, so that the paper looks like it did when you started. Now make the long folds again, one at a time, this time without folding the corners. Fold back the original corners, so that they sit on top of the folds. When you've done this your Diver should look like Illus. 205.

The dotted line across the nose in Illus. 205 shows where to make the next fold. When the nose fold is finished your Diver looks like Illus. 206. Now refold your paper airplane along its center fold so that it looks like Illus. 207.

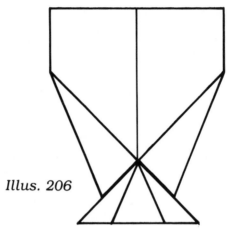

Illus. 206

Fold the near wing down on the dotted line in Illus. 207; then turn your Diver over and fold the other wing into place. At this stage your airplane is shown in Illus. 208.

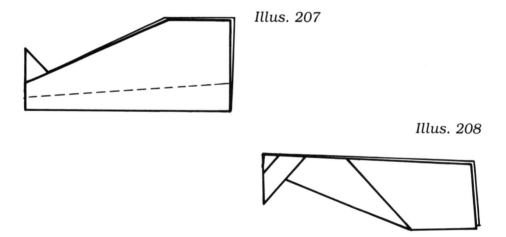

Illus. 207

Illus. 208

Open the wings into place and launch your Diver. You will discover that by holding the airplane closer to or farther from its nose will usually give it a slightly different flight path.

After a few flights change its trim by attaching a paper clip to its nose. Slip the clip over both sides of the fuselage. The change in trim and the fact that the fuselage's nose area is now held together will give Diver a longer glide and a faster one.

M.E. Special

The M.E. in M.E. Special stands for Modified Experimental, so, as you can guess, it's a changed design of an experimental plane.

For the M.E. Special you need two sheets of notebook paper, scissors and tape. Begin by cutting four pieces of material. The first should be 5 × 11 inches. The second piece needs to be 4 × 8 inches. Make the third piece of paper 1 × 6 inches, and finish up by cutting the fourth piece 4 × 5 inches.

Take the first paper you cut which will form the airplane's fuselage. With the long side facing you, fold the side over about ⅜ inch, as shown in Illus. 209. The dotted lines in that drawing indicate the folds you will make next. Keep folding the fuselage over and over until you have nothing left.

Once you have folded the final fold, use three strips of tape to fasten down the loose edge of the fuselage, so that it'll stay flat.

Now take the second piece of paper and, with the long side facing you, fold the edge over ½ inch. This is shown in Illus. 210. The two dotted lines show the next folds to make. Just fold the paper over twice. This gives you the leading edge of the midwing.

Fold one corner and crease it as shown in Illus. 211. Make sure it extends about ½ inch above the trailing edge of the wing. The dotted line shows where to make the next fold. Make this fold identical to the other one.

The midwing should now look like Illus. 212.

Fold both of the upper corners down as shown by the dotted lines in Illus. 213. Now make the two trailing edge

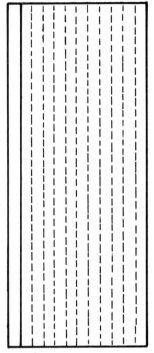

Illus. 209

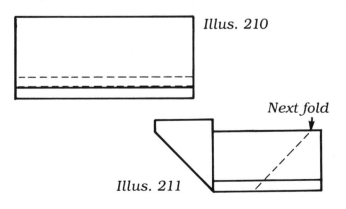

Illus. 210

Next fold

Illus. 211

Illus. 212

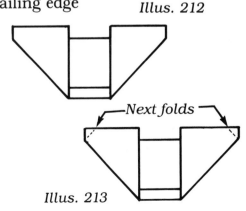

Next folds

Illus. 213

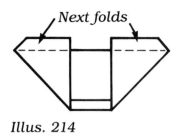

Illus. 214

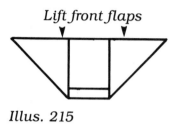

Illus. 215

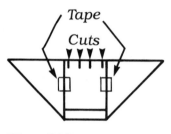

Illus. 216

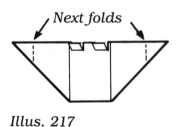

Illus. 217

folds as indicated by the dotted lines in Illus. 214. Crease these folds carefully into place.

Lift the two flaps of paper at the points shown by the arrows in Illus. 214. When you lift these flaps of paper, the two folds you just made will open a bit but the creases will stay in place.

Now refold the creases you made in Illus. 214 along their creases, but do this while the two front pieces are still up in the air. This will get the two trailing edges tucked in and out of the way so they will not interfere with your airplane's flight. Illus. 215 shows the trailing edge flaps tucked into place.

Now fold the front pieces back onto the wing. Use short pieces of tape to hold them down tightly. Illus. 216 shows you how. You should also see where to make four short cuts in the trailing edge. These are for control flaps. Make these cuts now.

Turn the midwing over and bend the two trailing edge flaps up a bit. Fold up on the dotted lines in Illus. 217 to form vertical stabilizers.

Set this piece aside and pick up the third piece of material. With the 5-inch side facing you, make a fold about ¾ inch wide and fold the paper over on itself until there is nothing left to fold; then fasten the loose edge in place with a strip of tape. The dotted lines in Illus. 218 show these folds.

Illus. 219 shows the folded forewing, and also shows where to fold up two more vertical stabilizers. Fold them up at the dotted lines.

Now let's deal with the last piece of paper. Form it into a loop and fasten the ends together with a small piece of tape. Illus. 220 shows the finished loop.

Illus. 218

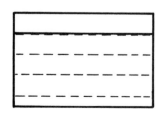

Illus. 219

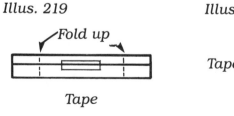

Illus. 220

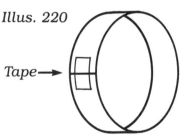

It's now time to assemble your M.E. Special. Lay the fuselage flat on the table, and place the three wing and stabilizer sections on top of the fuselage as shown in Illus. 221. Make sure you follow the measurements as nearly as possible. Tape the forewing in place so that its leading edge is 2 inches from the airplane's nose. Leave 2 inches between the trailing edge of this section and the leading edge of the midwing and tape the midwing securely onto the fuselage. The circular stabilizer should be taped into place about 1 inch from the airplane's tail.

To launch your M.E. Special place your index finger at the tip of the tail. Launch it as though you were throwing a dart.

If you needed to trim the nose with paper clips, clip them over the folded material so half the clip is inside the nose. Two clips, one on either side, should provide just the right amount of trim.

You should consider setting up paper airplane competitions with your friends. You may have already had some informal contests, but here are some competition categories you may want to consider.

Distance covered in a single flight is a popular contest. Just be sure if you hold this contest outdoors that the wind is blowing the same speed and from the same direction for all flights.

Acrobatics or loops and spins make up another good category. Compete for whose paper airplanes make the most loops in a single flight, or which model makes the most turns or changes in direction.

If you really get into these contests, don't be afraid to come up with your own categories.

You should also be thinking about designing some airplanes on your own. They can be modifications of models you have already built, but better yet, your ideas may be completely experimental.

Just remember that the worst that can happen to any paper airplane you build is that it won't fly, and remember, the world won't end if a project fails. Just take a minute to figure out what went wrong and then have another go at it.

Fly safely and have fun. That's what paper airplanes are all about.

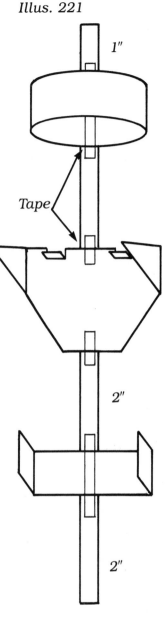

Illus. 221

Index